SWEET GRASS

Lives of Contemporary Native Women
of the Northeast

by
Mildred Noble

SWEET GRASS
Lives of Contemporary Native Women of the Northeast

© 1997 Mildred Noble

cover concept: Mildred Noble
cover painting: Michael McConnell
design: Judith Fuhring
photos: Cynthia Kulfan, Mainframe

send correspondence to:
C.J. Mills
224 Main Street
Mashpee, MA 02647

Table of Contents

This book is dedicated to
The Indian Community of Boston

Acknowledgments

I met many creative and wonderful people while working on Sweet Grass. Their friendship supported my effort to walk with determination on new paths and in new directions during the ten years it took to complete this book. To the men and women who were supportive of my cause during that time, my grateful thanks. Among them were Mary Brook, Shirley Mills, Pat Landry, Mishanagqus Mills, Raven and Bob Gustavson, Cynthia Kulfan, Jason Lang, Gary Linden, Peter DeRico and Angela, and Susan and Bruce Oakes.

I thank the women whose stories appear in this book and who replied most enthusiastically when I asked if I could interview them: "Yes! Okay! I am fed up reading negative articles and books written by people that simply do not understand our culture and where we are coming from!" I met Helen Manning in Boston at the Indian Commissioner's Task Force meeting in 1972. Later, in 1994, we were both honored as Elder Leaders of New England at a function hosted by the Native American Indian Awareness Program of New England. I knew Joanne Dunn, Rita Stevens, and Barbara Namias as coworkers at the Boston Indian Council (now renamed the Native American Community Center of Boston).

I am grateful to Dean Woods, my educational counselor at Boston College. Without his understanding and compassion I would not have furthered my education and certainly would not have changed course in my middle years to the extent that I have.

The interest of Mel King, Director of the Urban Fellowship Program at the Massachusetts Institute of Technology, in the effort to document life stories of Native women of the Northeast encouraged me to begin—and complete!—this project. To him I give my heartfelt thanks.

I salute Ed Prifogle, personal friend, technical advisor, and part-time editor, and extend my sincere thanks and gratitude to my friend and editor, Richard G. Carlson.

Introduction

We have a saying in Indian Country: *"Knowledge is passed down to the next seven generations ahead."*

In 1985 I initiated a process that led to my writing short autobiographical sketches of contemporary Indian women; in 1997 I have completed it. I started by jotting down notes of childhood experiences that I remembered during a stressful period of my life. Those memories unfolded in graphic pictures, almost as if I were looking through a kaleidoscope. Whether or not I had the technical ability to "write" was of no consequence. I just did.

In 1987 I graduated from Boston College with a Bachelor of Arts degree in social science. Several years later I submitted an application to Mel King, Director of the Urban Community Fellowship Program at the Massachusetts Institute of Technology. I was accepted into the program. While at M.I.T. as a Community Fellow, I embarked on several projects. One was to research my ancestry and the history of the Ojibway tribe, of which I am a member. That same year I interviewed "Rita" (whose story is in this book) and became acutely aware that information about Native American women—particularly those of the Northeast—was scarce and hard to locate.

There was a time during the writing of this book when I felt I could not go on. I was about to give up the idea completely. I had begun writing without ever contemplating what the end result would be. I was using writing as a therapeutic device. At one point, I hoped writing my story would give my daughter more understanding of her Indian mother.

My early efforts were written in a random and disorganized fashion, and, since I did not have the experience to rearrange it, the thought of completing the book was overwhelming to me. I contemplated this problem as I sat on a park bench, or watched TV, or walked about the city. I began to question the project's validity and whether I could finish it. "Why must I do it?" I asked myself. "What value is there in writing about Indian women's lives?" No answer. Time passed. Eventually I made a decision. I would finish what I started. Why not? Perhaps I could document life experiences as other writers had for Jewish women immigrants and the women of Appalachian Virginia and Tennessee. I devoured their stories and felt greatly empowered by the strength such women evoked. I determined to continue, therefore, documenting what contemporary life was like for Native American women. It was at this time that I met Richard Carlson, who assured me he would work with me in editing the stories.

In mid-life, out of necessity, I developed new skills. I tell in the following pages of practicing typing and the effort it took. Typing was a challenge, and I realize now that if I hadn't made that effort I would not have had the ability to follow through with other interests I later developed. I have also learned to use a computer as a word processor but only because at the first class I attended at Massachusetts Institute of Technology the instructor asked if everyone was computer literate. Since I was not, the "Green Room" (a room designated for computer practice) and tutors were made available to me as a Community Fellow. I was afraid of computers and remained freaked out the few times I summoned up enough courage to make it to the room. I was fearful of coming into contact with all the "brainy" people I might meet there. What would they think of me, an elder entering their ivory tower? Weeks passed before I got up courage to go in; even then, I just went several times and only because my instructor prodded me weekly. Needless to say, the young men and women I met there were kind and considerate, and I realize now that having that experience has helped me immensely in developing my skills as a writer.

The first part of this book—"Sweet Grass"—is my own story. The second part consists of briefly told lives of five Native American women—three Micmacs, one Mohawk, and one Wampanoag. Some of those stories have been fictionalized; others are presented as interviews which I conducted with them.

Millie Noble

1 ⚞

Millie's Story

I walked with my family on a path of hard crusted snow. A dog sled led the way. Bursts of energy shooting off in the sky lit up the earth like a giant fireworks display. Shimmering colors of pink, purple, and molten gold rippled cross the sky (the *aurora borealis*). Bitter cold winds stung my face.

I was two or thereabouts. I was tired. My legs hurt. Father picked me up and carried me. I heard his strained breathing and said to him, "Put me down."

My first recollections of life!

My Parents

I will begin.

I am Paibomsai. I was born in 1925 in a log cabin in the wilderness of Canada to parents who were band members of the Ojibway Nation. Mother was enrolled in a northern Ojibway band, and Father was allied with the Whitefish River Reserve in southern Ontario.

My parents met at "Bobbica," Mother's family homestead, in 1911 and were married that same year at Temagimi, a Cree reserve located 500 miles northeast of Toronto. Leaving their tribal connections behind, they went to live in an isolated area of northern Ontario, where cold weather and seasonal change dominated all else.

I was born when my parents were in their forties. I remember their black hair was slightly gray. But their eyes, looking out from warm, brown faces, were always bright with curiosity.

Mother was a tall, heavy-framed woman, whose radiant and welcoming smile revealed snagged teeth. With strangers she was timid and shy, and remained passive when discriminated against in town. With family members and other Indians, however, she was bright, cheerful, and generous to a fault, always sharing whatever food we had on hand.

Father had a charming personality—except for those times when he withdrew into himself and remained in a self-imposed silence for a day or two.

To assess my parents life through their exterior image would be false, however. Shabbily dressed, they revealed an air of stoicism. By the standards of mainstream society they would have been considered illiterate and uneducated. Of course, a person cannot be judged by appearance alone, and the true nature of an individual is hardly revealed with one glance.

I lived my first eighteen years with my parents, who followed a lifestyle of their own choosing. Most summers we roamed the isolated wilderness like vagabonds, canoeing the waterways of the northern tundra and living in a canvas tent. But during those same years we sometimes lived, for various reasons, on the outskirts of a small mining town, founded when gold was discovered in the subarctic in 1895. The town was populated principally by French-speaking people, but other ethnic groups—particularly English, Irish, and Scotch—also lived there. At the turn of the century, religious refugees from the Baltic countries settled in the town as well.

Sometimes Father met strangers and brought them home. These were the vagrant men of the 'thirties who traveled the country in railway boxcars. I can only guess why Father invited them home. I suppose it was for entertainment, since Father discussed issues of the day with them. Mother eagerly prepared supper for them, and both my parents enjoyed the strangers' conversation, listening intently as the men related their travel experiences.

Father also attended drinking gatherings in the town. One night he came home with a baby boy. Father had all daughters and I suppose he wanted a boy. The baby was six-months old when he came to live with us, the same age I was. He was a blond, with gray eyes and a fair skin. He was born to an unwed Indian girl who had been deserted. Father met the girl's brother at the party, and it was arranged that my parents would care for him. My parents raised him as their own.

I also had two sisters. One was ten years older than I, the other four years older. They both contracted tuberculosis when they were teenagers. At different times each was sent to a sanitarium 300 miles from home for treatment. I was sixteen when one died, twenty when the other died.

When Mother and Father were victimized by racial injustices in the town, they remained passive. They accepted the condition. I cannot help but think that sometimes the experience of being victims highlighted their lives. Whenever they were affected and overpowered by the townspeople's racist attitudes, my parents rushed back to a familiar place—the bush country—with a zestful and joyous attitude.

When we lived in the town, my parents obeyed the local laws; when we lived in the country, they were close to nature and the spiritual law of the land. My parents' strength of character enabled them to survive in both worlds. They enjoyed life and had the power to hold fast to that idea in either place. With grace and dignity, for all the many years of their lives, they adapted to the dynamics their two different lifestyles demanded.

Mother's brother and sister lived in the same small town with their families, but we never celebrated occasions with them and they never accompanied us on our summer trips. I was fond of my aunt, who had a knack for making the best *bannock* (Indian biscuits). She sometimes attempted to curl my straight, black hair using curlers she made by cutting strips of paper from brown paper bags. Mother's sister married a French-Canadian. Their children were all fair-complexioned with brown hair. My family was brown-skinned and black-haired. I was never close to my cousins.

Grandfather traveled back and forth between Bobbica and town according to the seasons. In the summer months he worked the garden at the family homestead, continuing to supply his family with potatoes until his death at age eighty. In town, he lived in a small cabin. Because he no longer trapped or hunted, he was not harassed by the town police as my father was.

Wherever we were, my parents always worked together. Survival depended on such a relationship. Side-by-side, they never seemed to intrude or invade each other's space. The effort to share work was based on team spirit and team effort. Both parents had been taught Indian customs and values; with such knowledge they had the skills to survive the harsher elements of the wilderness. Spiritually, they balanced their lives to exist in harmony with the earth.

Our family homestead was in the bush country. Sometimes we staked out an abandoned cabin in the wilderness for the season or traveled the waterways of the northern tundra. One summer Father even stayed in town and worked at the local sawmill, and one winter he guided a surveying team. These were the only paying jobs that I recall he had. Usually he provided for his family by hunting and fishing. He also received a semi-annual "treaty check" from his reserve in the amount of six dollars for each family member.

Father knew the rutting season for animals. When he went moose hunting he rolled birchbark into a horn. As dusk settled over the countryside, we patiently sat in a canoe and waited. Father blew out a raucous mating call. Generally a moose responded by crashing through the brush. After it was killed, my parents prepared its hide for use. It was a long, painstaking process. Father scraped hair from the hide before tanning it over smoke from the campfire. Mother made moccasins and leggings from the pliable skin, using sinew from the muscle of the moose as thread to sew clothing. My parents prepared the meat by smoking it over a campfire.

Father also snared rabbits and tanned their skins, while Mother made rabbit stew and wove the rabbit skins into blankets. In the winter months she spent many evenings painstakingly sewing small stitches by the yellow glow of a lamplight. One winter I remember she also wove a fish net, but Father used it only occasionally.

Father was not only a hunter and fisher; he was also a storyteller. Whenever family or others gathered, he told tales of "Nannabush" and other Ojibway legends. He spoke of sailing on the Great Lakes and other activities that took place in the warmer climate of southern Ontario.

Sometimes he recalled his own adventures when he went off to Toronto, boasting to family and friends that he was going to be a "city Indian." Alas! What skills he brought with him were not the ones he needed to survive there. Father knew what his father had taught him: how to hunt and fish; how to construct snowshoes and canoes; how to choose the right herbal roots to make Indian medicine. But in 1895 Toronto needed skilled craftsmen and factory workers. Father was too embarrassed to return to his reserve, so he traveled north to the Hudson Bay region of the province—north to his destiny, if you will. There he spent the next forty years.

When he was seventy he was alone. My mother died at age seventy and my two sisters when they were in their twenties. I was ill in the United States and had lost contact with him. He then returned to the land of his birth, to his reserve. There he spent the remaining years of his life with family and friends.

Father's Family Tree

GRANDFATHER PAIBOMSAI, 1769

Somewhere between the dream world and the light and dark of life, Paibomsai was slowly awakening to full consciousness. As he returned to the light, he heard the whispers of the red rose petals fluttering in the wind and felt the heaviness of the morning dew on him. When he finally opened his eyes his vision was blurred. The flickering yellow that filtered in through the leafy branches added to the dreamlike quality of his re-entry to the world.

Paibomsai heard the faint sound of willow flutes and knew that the Elders were coming for him. He stretched his limbs and cautiously moved his body about the huge rock on which he lay, curved to accommodate his body by generations of shamans who had come there before him. Finally he sat up.

How long had he lain there? On his first night the full moon had reassured him by its presence. Then many days and nights passed until another full moon appeared. Last night, the tiny sliver of light of the quarter moon had beckoned him to take up life again. He had successfully completed the ritual of fasting and meditation.

Rising from the creche, he greeted the Elders of the tribe who climbed the long steep hill. They stood in a circle around him, waiting for his signal for their help. Then they assisted him down the hill and to his lodge, where he slowly sipped the porcupine broth they prepared for him.

As the hot liquid slipped slowly down his throat, Paibomsai felt restored. His body was strong and powerful again. But his mind continued to whirl with the visions and images he must reveal to the tribe after he had rested and meditated. He would have to sort these out and consult with an Elder on the true nature of his vision quest.

The next day, Paibomsai awakened to the light of the morning sun. Walking slowly to the lodge of the medicine man, he prepared to speak of the message he had received.

"I was on the crest of a hill overlooking a village," he told the medicine man. "In my vision I could see inside a lodge, and I heard a man and woman speaking of their son, a boy of seven who lay sleeping. The mother gently covered him with a fur robe. The parents spoke in happiness to each other, and the father said, 'I want him to be the strongest warrior in the land of the Cree and Ojibway.' 'I will nurture him well,' said the mother.

"The parents continued to talk and plan their son's future. His father said, 'I will train him to become the fastest runner, and he will win at wrestling matches, and at the swimming races.' The parents both agreed that they would be pleased if he became the leader and chief of their village."

Paibomsai told the medicine man that he watched time evolve, that he saw the boy grow tall, and that he was happy when the elders of the village laughed at the boy's stories. As the father stood sternly nearby and watched, his son danced to the beating of the drum and chanted the music of the Ojibway people.

Paibomsai had also seen puzzlement on the father's face as the boy continued as a singer, dancer, and storyteller. And the father was not pleased when his son did not win in any games. The boy, who was slight of build, had a competitive spirit, but it was not enough for him to be victorious in anything he attempted.

The medicine man listened as Paibomsai continued to speak.

"The father told his son, "It is time for your vision quest to begin." The father hoped the boy would win some games or show signs of becoming a leader of his people. The boy undertook the quest when he was fourteen. He did not receive a vision on that first attempt, however. He tried again each year for the next four years, but the result was always the same.

"On the fifth try, the father again brought the boy to Cradle Rock, and left him there as was the custom. But when he returned in four days he did not see his son and could not find him. The father looked all around the area, but his son had disappeared. As the father searched for his son, he heard a little bird, singing and hopping nearby. The bird's red breast and black beak were beautiful to look at, and its singing and chirping lightened the man's heart. The bird became his constant companion as he searched vainly for his son.

"Desolate, the father eventually returned to his lodge. The bird, chirping alongside, accompanied him. Each morning it awakened the father with song; at nighttime it stayed close by. The father was never alone. But his son never returned.

"Many years later, when the father lay near death, he heard the sound of his son's voice coming from the bird. 'I never left you, Father.'

"This is what I have to say to the people of the village; they may interpret it as they wish."

GREAT-GRANDFATHER ANDREW PAIBOMSAI, 1850

Andrew Paibomsai, "Chief" of the Whitefish River Reserve and member of the Grand Council of Chiefs of the Ojibway Nation, was one of the signers of the Robinson Huron Treaty (1850). This treaty, including amendments, continues to be enforced by the Canadian Government. The treaty established British authority over the Ojibway tribes and provided for the enumeration of all tribal members, who were given band numbers. Since then, any offspring of tribal members who chose to live off the reserve have been known to the tribe by their ancestors' names and numbers that were recorded. In 1850 Great–grandfather Andrew Paibomsai was registered with the Whitefish River Reserve.

The Robinson Huron Treaty did not recognize any special rights for women. Indeed, the law often discriminated against women. For example, the children of native women who married non–Indian men could not be registered on tribal rolls and were not legally recognized as Indians. Men, however, could marry whom they wished, Indian or non–Indian, and their children would automatically be registered with a tribe and legally recognized as Indians. The discrepancy has been explained as follows. Prior to the Robinson Treaty land grants were awarded to Indians. It was apparently feared that white men who married Indian women would automatically became tribal members, gain full Indian status, and become landowners and voting members of a tribe. In 1985, after seven years of effort, the Métis women of Canada brought about the repeal of this law. The descendants of women affected by this act in 1850 have since regained Indian status.

ANDREW PAIBOMSAI, 1881

My grandfather, Andrew Paibomsai, established a small store on the reserve where he sold basic provisions: needles, thread, canned milk, tea, sugar, and some clothing. Andrew could not read or write. When ordering supplies from Eaton's, a mail–order catalog, he drew whatever merchandise he needed.

An Ojibway elder whom I interviewed, a woman of ninety, told me the following story about my grandfather and the friends and relatives who came to his store. Gesturing with her hands as if she was holding something, she said, "They would carry out large cans of milk in their hands and would not pay him. They had no money." The woman smiled as she spoke and had a gleam in her eye. "The boat that brought the treaty money brought a peddler, too. He sold and got cash money for his goods. Your grandfather didn't get paid."

EDWARD PAIBOMSAI

In 1880, the year my father, Edward Paibomsai, was born, 250 tribal members lived on the reserve. For them, life continued to change. Missionaries who came to the area in 1860 built a church on the reserve. In 1901 a railroad was constructed. A mill constructed in 1860 was producing large quantities of lumber for Canada's expanding cities. Eventually the people on the reserve had access to this lumber for their own homes, and the first 10 x 12–foot wood–framed huts were built for them. These were in use until 1948, when larger ranch-style homes were crafted and built on the reserve.

Prior to the Robinson Huron Treaty (1850), traders reached the southern Ojibway country by traveling the Great Lakes of Ontario, a route used since the seventeenth century when the first fur traders ventured out from settlements in eastern Canada. It is interesting to note that among the earliest items of trade were bricks of maple sugar. The Indians of southern Ontario had known how to process maple sugar since time began. It has been documented that the Caribbean islands could not supply enough sugar. Thus, when the traders arrived in Indian territory and discovered maple sugar, it became in great demand. Eventually, the people new to this country organized the production of maple sugar into a thriving industry.

The pioneers and missionaries who arrived in North America as early as the sixteenth century wandered throughout Ojibway territory. Guided by Indians, they traveled the waterways in canoes designed and constructed by native people.

The missionaries zealously converted the red men to Christianity, even though some European philosophers said the Anishinabe ("the people of the earth") were without souls. But some Indians rejected conversion, saying to those who attempted it, "I will follow in my father's path and in his footsteps. I will stay forever on that path."

Indians, however, welcomed the tea, flour, cooking utensils, and tools that traders brought to them For centuries, the native women had used birchbark baskets as cooking utensils, adding hot stones to heat the water in the baskets. This was an alternative to cooking food over a blazing campfire.

The Anishinabe trained from childhood to study the earth, stars, moon, and sun. These were known to them as "all my relations". The shamans, also known as medicine men, had vast knowledge of the plants and vegetation of their particular region. They knew what roots and berries provided nutritional value or could be used in the treatment of various illnesses. Trained in what today we call physiology and psychology, shamans were healers and spiritual leaders of their tribe. The men, women, and children of the tribe were all skilled hunters and fishermen and provided food for themselves and the aging members of their community. The artists—singers, storytellers, and dancers—were also highly valued, as were the craftspeople who designed clothing, snowshoes, lodges, and canoes. Art was incorporated into both utilitarian and functional objects.

The Chief and members of his Grand Council, including women elders, were elected to their position by a democratic process; as such they were the decision-makers of their tribe and enforced tribal law.

Indians have survived because they have superb knowledge of their world. It was they, in fact, who saved the adventurers from coming to some sad end in the strange country where they traveled.

In researching Ojibway history I read journals written in the 18th century by men who traveled the wilderness as agents of their country. With disbelief I read their negative images of the people they encountered during their travels in the New World. It is difficult for me to understand their mindset or to comprehend their ignorance in recording that the indigenous people and their society were without value.

The men who wrote such ignorant facts about a people they barely knew did so as they were sitting in a canoe constructed and paddled by Indians. The Indians taught the strangers how to survive! Indians taught them how to fish and hunt, and even healed them with Indian medicine. The Ojibway women, who were nurturing helpmates to the strangers, were cast out and scorned by the invader's society.

Indians supplied provisions for the army in the French and English wars. They had to, for the soldiers who came from the cities and villages in Europe had little knowledge of the earth and animals, and did not know how to hunt or fish.

Some Indians even joined in the warfare, including one of my ancestors. Just recently, the youth of the Whitefish First Nation Reserve documented the story of a Paibomsai who enlisted in the army in the French and English war. They learned that he left behind a young wife. When he returned several years later, he learned that a baby had been born. When the child was young he spent many hours in the sun tanning himself, in hopes of being as brown as his brothers and sister.

Mother's Family Tree

DIAZA: GRANDMOTHER FIVE GENERATIONS PAST

Diaza heard strange sounds coming into her space. When she realized the sounds were coming from the direction of the river, she left her shelter to investigate. Standing high on the riverbank, she saw a canoe coming around the bend of the river. Two other canoes soon followed. In them were creatures whose faces, like birchbark, were covered with long shaggy hair. Diaza heard harsh, animal-like voices. Their strange guttural tones frightened her. There was no one with her to allay her fears.

Then Diaza noticed a human being, an Indian, in one of the canoes. He was sitting point, guiding the strangers through the wilderness waters.

Diaza knew her parents would be coming for her that day, for she had scratched three marks on the ground. Three days earlier her parents had left her alone on the point of a river with a small amount of food, a birchbark basket, a lighting stick, and a fur robe. There she would undertake a ritual that would mark her entrance into womanhood.

For three days and nights Diaza had lain inside a shelter she constructed by herself. Alone in the dark, she faced the terror of the unknown. She heard animals thrashing about and those sounds frightened her. She thought if she remained still and did not move the wolves or bears would not catch her scent. She did not leave the shelter until she heard the strange voices coming from the river.

She was twelve years old and the year was 1768.

The strangers whom Diaza saw that day were men of Hudson's Bay Company, the vanguard of the fur traders who would penetrate the northern wilderness of present-day Ontario Province.

Diaza was the first of her tribe to see white man enter Ojibway territory.

A century after Diaza undertook this rite of passage, the

Ojibways determined it was too harsh an ordeal for young women to undergo. The ritual included the bringing of young women of the Ojibway tribe to a point in a river or a lake by their parents; where they were left alone to deal with the perils of the unknown for a period of three day. Many young women perished. A great-great-great grandmother on my mother's side was the last woman of my Ojibway descendants to have undergone the ritual.

The story I have related has come down to my generation through oral translation. I heard it first when I was twelve or there-abouts while traveling the waterways of Canada with my parents. When I was approaching my twelfth birthday, I heard Mother teasingly exclaim many times as we passed a clearing in the river or a lake where the sandy beaches beckoned. "It looks like a nice place to leave you." I remember being terrified at the thought. She often related the story of Diaza, the first of her tribe to meet the white men of the Hudson's Bay Company. I suppose it can be related now as a myth or a legend. Because there is no documentation... But somewhere in my ancestral Ojibway past there was a young women who dared to undergo the rigorous advent into womanhood and survive.

GREAT-GRANDFATHER MOORE

Thomas Moore left his homeland in Scotland in 1827 to travel to Canada. He was twenty when he arrived and was but one of many young men who came to the New World that year to work for the Hudson's Bay Company. He was assigned to Moosenee, a post on the shores of James Bay in Ontario, Canada—Northern Ojibway and Cree territory prior to the discovery of America. Moose Factory, Moosenee's twin community, is one of Ontario's oldest settlements.

Mother's tribe, the Northern Ojibway, was a vital link in the development of the "fur trade society" which came into existence with the Hudson's Bay Company's rise to power. The Ojibway women, versed in all aspects of survival in the northern climes, assisted the Europeans to make the transition to life on the rugged frontier of the New World. The Hudson's Bay Company's policy relating to employee interactions with Native women changed with each century. In the eighteenth century, missionaries arrived at the company's posts and performed marriages between Indian women and European men.

When Thomas Moore arrived at Moosenee in 1827, he pursued and married Mary Diaza, a descendant of Diaza, the young woman who was the first Ojibway to meet the white man. A son, Joseph, was born in 1829. When Joseph was twenty he followed in his father's footsteps by both marrying a young woman from the Ojibway tribe and working as a runner for the Hudson's Bay Company.

In the nineteenth century, Moosenee was a thriving community despite its isolation and its subarctic temperatures. French, and English trappers arrived at the fort to celebrate and to obtain the essential supplies. Ships sailed through the icy waters of Hudson Bay into the lower James Bay to collect furs and to bring trade goods to the isolated community. (During the height of the slaughter of the buffalo on the western plains, the ships brought pickled buffalo tongues, a real delicacy at the fort.)

The fort's hierarchical social structure separated the Native and non-Native people, and Thomas and Joseph Moore, both Company employees, were allied with the Indian community. Joseph's spiritual and ethical beliefs, therefore, were shaped by Indian teachings. As a Company employee, however, he was obliged to follow its policy of discrimination toward the Cree and Ojibway people. The conflict that resulted shaped Joseph's thinking and social identity.

By the time he had worked for the Company for ten years, Joseph Moore had sired four daughters and one son. His wife and children spoke the language of the Ojibway; they did not read or write English and only spoke it when absolutely necessary. As teenagers, his daughters worked for Company families as household maids. They observed the customs of their employers and learned the finer skills of household etiquette and the use of the sewing machine to sew muslin blouses and serge skirts for themselves. They coiled their hair into high pompadours, the fashion of the time. They also used glass beads imported from Czechoslovakia to sew the emblem of the Ojibway Nation, a floral design, on their moccasins and other clothing.

Grandfather Joseph left his job and the settlement in 1889. As his descendant, I find it difficult to write about his experience which was told in oral tradition. Now I am breaking tradition by passing it down in the written word to my descendants.

One winter a fierce blizzard blasted through the north country. The huge amount of snow that fell during the storm literally covered the houses in the settlement and the Indians lodges outside the fort. The native people could not get out to fish in the bay or hunt. They were without food and were starving. Joseph Moore recognized how desperate the situation was. Since he was a company employee and had access to foodstuffs, he opened a pork barrel and distributed the contents to the people. For this compassionate action he was severely reprimanded by Company officials.

Angry and disillusioned by the Hudson's Bay Company's handling of this critical situation, Joseph concluded that Company policy lacked moral and ethical values in dealing with the Indians. He was so disgusted that he quit the Company and the community and moved his family to an isolated area three hundred miles from the nearest trading post or Indian settlement. In the nineteenth century, as was the custom, Queen Victoria's Canadian government awarded Joseph a land grant of four acres in the northern wilderness of Canada.

Joseph Moore left the settlement in the spring of 1889 with his wife and five offspring. Traveling in three canoes loaded down with the provisions and tools needed to start a new life, they searched the rivers, lakes and creeks of northern Ontario for a suitable place to settle. They finally came to a point in a river that led into a lake. They settled there and named their homestead "Bobbica", which in the Ojibway language means "where the waters meet."

The first year they were there, the family cleared a portion of land and constructed a log cabin. On their first trip to the nearest settlement they brought back glass for windows.

Grandfather had little knowledge of farming and carpentry but what skills he had he used to improve the homestead. He made a root house by digging soil from the slope of a hill. In the winter he cut blocks of ice from the lake and stored them there in packs of sawdust for use during the summer months.

The family's diet followed the seasons. They planted potatoes and picked berries that grew wild and dried them in the hot summer days. They hunted and fished, then smoked and salted fish and game. They tanned the skins to make moccasins and clothing; rabbit skins were woven into blankets. Grandfather and his family skillfully constructed toboggans and snowshoes, and carved bone to make blades for ice skates. These items were essential to maintain their lifestyle.

Occasionally the family made trips to visit Indian settlements and buy basic essentials. On one occasion, the daughters, all bush country Indians, were photographed dressed in white muslin shirts and serge skirts, their hair coiffed in the nineteenth century pompadour style.

The daughters were in their twenties and had been living at "Bobbica" in their isolated environment for ten years when gold was discovered in the Canadian sub-arctic, an event that altered the family's pattern of life forever. Across the lake from "Bobbica" a hydroelectric plant was built to provide power for a new town down river. The family was soon interacting with the construction workers.

One of Joseph Moore's daughters married a Frenchman, while another never married. A third daughter, an unwed mother, died in childbirth. My own mother, Mary Moore, met an Ojibway trapper who paddled up from the lakes and rivers of southern Ontario. They were married on the Temagimi Reserve in 1911.

The Seasons

SUMMER IN THE WILDERNESS

Why my family wandered on the waterways of the north country I can only guess. Perhaps it was something for them to do. We traveled in two canoes carrying just the basics: a tent, blankets, cooking pots, food, and a change of clothing. Besides my parents and myself, there were my adopted brother, the sister who was four years older than I (we no longer went on the summer trips after my second sister died), and a cousin on my mother's side. Some summers we went north to visit isolated Indian villages located near James Bay. Other summers we hunted and fished on the nearby lakes and rivers.

During our canoe trips we battled strong currents in the rock strewn rivers and crossed lakes that sparkled from the reflections of the azure blue sky. When we came to an unusual grouping of rocks spread over the wild terrain my parents would stop paddling the canoe to rest and observe the spectacular sight. The gray basalt rocks sometimes looked as if they had been sculptured and thrown recklessly to the ground. My imagination soared. Animals etched in stone were keeping watch over the silent countryside. Other massive stones looked as if they had been carved into geographic lines and abstract forms. (Looking at rocks as art forms was a Native Americans practice, but I was unaware of it until after I had written of doing just that with my family.)

When we stopped for lunch at the foot of a slope or steep hill, Father urged us to climb to the top. He, of course, always led the way. At the summit we gazed at the terrain below. Blue ribbons of color meandered around the green landscape. The trunks of white birch trees scattered among the green foliage dazzled the eye with intense light.

RAPIDS

I have sharp, clear images of traveling down a river one hot day in July. I was five years old, my short black hair was cut in bangs, and I was wearing a white flour bag shimmy dress that Mother had made it the previous winter. I was sitting in my usual place in the gunwale of the canoe, where I fit neatly because of my small size. From that position I could look up and out at the world.

As the canoe glided quietly along the gentle river, I daydreamed and let my fingers trail in the water. To escape the heat of the sun we paddled close to shore under hanging branches that lined the riverbank. Light breezes stirring the air intertwined with musky smells and summer noises. The amber glow of the lazy afternoon spread across the earth in shadowed spaces. Up ahead trees were mirrored in the water. I watched how the illusion shattered into pieces as the canoe surged forward. But the river, pulsing with excitement, still wove a magic spell. From the matted under-brush came flashing black and yellow color. Summer bees rushed out to greet us, but paddling quickly, we left them spinning in the amber light.

Alongside the riverbank, pink and white flowers swayed gently in the summer wind. Overhead, birds flipped their agile wings and landed on gray logs jutting from the river bed. As we passed close by, I stared into beady, feral eyes and saw just blank spots of light. Wet brown beavers surfaced, then quickly smacked their flat tails hard and dove back down to their watery homes.

Suddenly, in the distance ahead of us, I heard the sound of water breaking. I sighed. I knew that rapids lay ahead. (Any large rapids we encountered on these summer trips were portaged around.)

We paddled around a bend in the river and just as quickly came to the rushing water. Father called out, "Mary, we have to pull over to change places." Mother, looking ahead, answered, "It doesn't look too bad from here." Father steered the canoe over to the bank of the river, where we rested as my parents assessed the strength and power of the currents in the river. When we got back in the canoe, Mother went to the stern. There she would steer the craft through the white water. Father took his place in the bow.

As we entered the rapids the strong currents instantly seized our canoe and sent it spinning. It careened toward the jagged rocks. We were out of control but Father acted quickly. Over the water's noise, I heard his voice shout a sharp command. "Don't move!" Seizing his paddle, he stood up and, with strong deft hands, shoved us away from the jagged rocks. I sensed Father's fear—and his energy.

I was directly in front of him, in the gunwale, peering out and seeing up close the chaotic maelstrom of water swirling around. I was so petrified I closed my eyes. The water splashed hard against the rocks and bounced off them in high sprays. Brilliant cascades then flowed back down and thoroughly drenched us as we passed through this violent mass of power. Looking behind me, I saw Mom's face, red and taut from the effort she was making to steer the canoe.

In the midst of the tumultuous waters it seemed as if time stood still. Eventually, of course, the water trailing in sudsy circles around our canoe became smaller. We left the space and moved into quieter waters. We were through. Our energy spent, Father commented, "Well, it was not too bad. We will stop soon for the night."

I now realize that the rapids we safely rode out that July day so long ago were actually small ones—although still highly volatile. Seen from a child's perspective, they were, of course, awesome.

Later that afternoon, Father hollered, "Let's break for camp. That spot over there looks good." He steered the canoe over to the bank, where dry rust pine needles littered the ground. The fragrant smell of pine trees was everywhere in the air. We pitched our tent in the midst of them. Father ambled about ordering his three children to "pick small branches off the trees and pile them in the tent." Then he ordered us, "Go pick wood for the fire. Be sure to bring some dry rot wood back."

Father prepared Mother's outdoor kitchen. He cut sturdy branches from an elm tree, whittled them into a pole, then canted them over the fire at a forty-five degree angle. Mother hung pots on them to boil water for tea and to cook potatoes. In the midst of cooking utensils spread on the ground, she kneaded bannock dough and prepared the fish we had caught earlier that day. She gutted, scaled and fried the fish in a black iron skillet over the red coals of the campfire. After Father mumbled his incantations of prayer we ate our evening meal sitting on logs and balancing the plates on our laps.

When my sister Jane said, "Let's go for a swim," we raced to the river. There we encountered mosquitoes and black flies that emerged into the air spontaneously with the rosy glow of sunset.

When we swam, Father had swished around a smudge pot of acrid smoke that still lingered when we returned. After closing the flaps of the tent, I fell asleep to the mysterious stirrings of the earth—an animal thrashing about and a owl hooting somewhere close by.

When I awoke in the gray light of morning I again listened to the stirring of Mother Earth. Leaves rustled in the wind. Birds chirped—softly at first and then, by ancient design, more loudly as they alerted all living creatures to respond! A loon sang its sad lament, a haunting cry floating over the wild celebration chorus of other sounds.

I ran to the river and stood on the sandy beach. While the water lapped gently at my feet, I washed. On the opposite shore the sun rose high over a jagged tree line. White mist skimmed the top of the water and evaporated, revealing patches of blue water sparkling in the sun. A pencil-thin streak of yellow light blazed toward me.

Smoke from the campfire drifted in the air. I ran back to the campsite. Mother had boiled blueberries and fried salt pork, and a bannock was baking on the gray coals of the campfire. We each dipped our bread in the grease of the salt pork and the blueberry sauce. We drank our tea hot and black and from tin cups.

After breakfast we broke camp. Using sand as soap, we washed our dishes and cooking utensils in the river. Then we stowed our gear in the canoe and pushed off for another day on the water.

Cloudbursts and rainstorms came up suddenly while we were on these trips. Father had an instinct—an innate sense of when a storm lurked in the distance. He always stopped paddling the canoe to scrutinize the sky, holding his head in a way that suggested intense thought. When the sky darkened and the winds stilled, we made a hasty break for shore. There, we quickly tipped the canoe over and huddled together under it until the storm had passed. The rains came, thunder crashed, the earth shook. Lightning streaked across the sky. Gray mist rose and swirled around like murky fog on the wet steamy earth. After the storm was spent, we crawled from our shelter, stood up, inhaled the clean fresh air, and continued on our way.

It was autumn when we returned. The monotonous green countryside had turned into a barrage of color: crimson leaves with flecks of yellow, dazzling orange with touches of brown and yellow ocher. The array of color swirling around us touched our spirits.

We walked through the brush stepping on leaves that were blown to the earth by the gusty winds of fall. Each family member carried supplies. I trudged along the path, carrying in each hand tin pails filled with food. Father carried the canoe on his back. We went to sleep in a tent that was cold and damp and woke in the morning to find it covered with slivers of ice.

SCHOOL DAYS IN TOWN

After I was fourteen, my family no longer went on summer trips, but usually stayed in town or at the family homestead.

As a school kid I compared myself to my classmates. I had straight, coarse black hair but longed for curly hair. The other girls in class wore bright-colored sweaters and skirts and wore shoes (covered by galoshes in winter!). Mother made my clothes for me from dark, used clothing. I wore moccasins most of the time, although I did get to wear a pair of sneakers occasionally.

Throughout the few short years I attended school, I experienced racial attacks from adults and children in the town. At the turn-of-the-century refugees fleeing religious persecution in Europe had come to this town. It is ironic that it was their children who later persecuted my family and me with racial slurs.

When school let out the other children walked home with each other. Their laughter rang out in the cold clear air. I walked home alone. Sometimes the kids noticed me and taunted me. "*Savages! Savages !*" That cry lingered in my head long after the episode was over. Throughout the winter they enthusiastically threw snowballs and ice at me. They never let up. They showed no mercy. In the spring and summer they threw rocks at me and splattered me with mud.

I fled from such attacks. When I reached home, trembling and crying after an aggressive encounter with them, I would fling open the kitchen door and cry out to Mom," Why do they do that to me?" She never answered or consoled me, although once she blurted out, "It is because we are Indian." I never asked the question again.

Because they were usually so cruel to me, I was surprised when some classmates invited me to an afternoon school program held at a local church. Excited, I asked my parents' permission to join them.

It was a cold day in late autumn when I made my way to the church. The first snowfall had sprinkled a dusting of snow. I entered a warm, cozy hall, where hardwood floors were polished to a fine finish, making them shine with a soft gleam. The chairs formed a semi-circle. The teacher, an elder with soft white curls around her wrinkled face, sat waiting. She prepared the class for instruction. Given a hoop, colored thread, and a piece of etched material to work with, I sprawled in my chair and energetically sewed small stitches as neatly as I could. Suddenly, I was startled to hear the teacher speak to me in harsh tones. She ordered me to sit up straight. I quickly pulled my feet in and sat up straight and proper.

After class I went home and announced proudly to my family, "I am learning how to do embroidery work. Ha! Ha!" and wiggled with excitement.

The following week I found the teacher waiting at the door. She would not allow me to enter, but said, "You can't come in. You are not a member of this class."

I was dumbfounded as I stood in the doorway before her. I sensed her aged presence and saw clearly the dusting of talcum powder sprinkled on her wrinkled neck. Wafts of lilac fragrance drifted from her. Later, when cosmetics were accessible to me, I developed an allergy to such fragrances.

I was nine years old when I left the public school system. My last day of school began like any other day. It was springtime and the sun shone brightly. The snow melted fast, and as I walked to school in the slush I had no inkling that my world was about to crash down around me. When I entered the classroom my wet and soggy moccasins made squishy noises as I walked to my seat at the back of the room. A steam radiator next to me was steaming, making hissing and clanking noises. The teacher called my name. I stood up and heard her say, "Mildred, go home and take a bath. You stink !"

I was shocked. Had I heard right? I could not believe I actually heard what she said. I fell into my seat and could not move. I could not leave the room. The other kids were staring at me. A blanket of silence filled the room. I finally moved, but with each step I took toward the door I wanted to shrink out of sight. I became physically ill after that episode and never returned to school again. My family returned to the bush country.

Forty years passed before I entered a classroom again, this time as a participant in an alcoholism training program at Boston City Hospital. At that time I don't know if I consciously or subconsciously remembered this experience. There were so many dehumanizing actions directed toward me and my family, I probably did not have the energy to separate them out.

Strangely, however, when I looked out the window that bleak, rainy day in Boston, memories of that childhood incident came whooshing in. I found myself trying to rationalize the teacher's actions. Perhaps wet moose-skin moccasins did indeed give out an unpleasant odor when drying out in a warm, crowded room. I thought of the teacher who long ago had come from the wheat fields of Manitoba to teach the kids in the far north country. Miss Ames was a tall, lanky woman with stringy brown hair that fell in wisps around her homely face. She often wore a forest green tweed suit and she taught me to read.

Winter Wolves

As I sit by a lake on Cape Cod and hear the tinkling sound of water lapping at my feet, I am seduced, taken out of the realities of today and into voices and echoes of another time.

I am back in Canada. It is winter. In the rosy glow of the lamp-light that circles the table, I see again how my parents reacted when I told them of my day's adventure.

"I saw wolves today," I announced abruptly.

My parents stopped talking. My father's face expressed concern. "Where?" he asked. My mother looked dismayed as she waited for my answer.

"They were down in the clearing, you know where," I answered.

Earlier that day, after a snowstorm's fiendish, howling winds and frigid blasts of arctic air had come and gone, I had ventured out of our cabin to see what havoc had been wrought. Perhaps a tree had sprung from its roots to land lopsidedly in the snow. The snow drifts were piled into mysterious forms and looked like visions of frozen objects that had crashed into space. As I walked along I felt the cold, bitter air sting my face. When I came to the clearing in the woods I stumbled.

Just as I was falling to the ground, a pack of wolves came into the clearing from the other side. I did not move. The wolves stopped and grouped at the clearing's edge. Suddenly they threw their heads back, opened their mouths wide, and howled. The blood–curdling sounds reverberated in the frozen air.

I lay still in the snow and hoped the wolves would not catch my scent. Eventually they turned and went quietly back into the brush. I got up. A snowflake drifted. The air was still. The surface of the clearing reflected the sky like a tapestry of blue crystal ice. I turned and ran. Digging my moccasins into the snow, I heard distinctly the crunching sounds they made as I fled to the safety of my home.

A Winter Trip to Town

When we spent the winter in the bush country, my family usually made a trip to town to pick up our treaty check at the local post office and get basic supplies to last the winter. We always looked forward to making the trip, despite the hardship of walking thirty miles on the ice and snow in below-zero temperatures. We also expected encounter the townspeople's racial attitudes and to hear racial slurs thrown at us by the kids of the town.

We left in the early morning while it was still dark in order to get to town by late afternoon. Often a yellow disk hung low in the sky. We walked single file behind the dog-sled carrying our supplies. As we came close to town sometimes we kids hitched a ride on a horse-drawn sleigh.

On this particular day, we arrived in town late. The house was cold, bitterly cold. Mother quickly got a fire going in the black iron stove. She bustled around the room, preparing supper by bringing out two frozen rabbits from the shed and putting them in a pot to cook. The aroma of rabbit stew soon filled the warm room.

We sat down to our evening meal. Father gave thanks to the Great Spirit for the food and for our safe journey. In the glow of the lamplight, we sat around the table, laughing and talking despite our fatigue.

The temperature outside was below zero and the night air was silent. Suddenly we heard the sound of a motor. Tires crunched in the snow. I watched the expressions on my parents' faces change from happiness to apprehension. They whispered to each other, "It is the police." Fear filled the room.

We stopped chattering and listened intently. I was terrified. My whole family waited in silence for something to happen. Endless moments passed before the disruption began. Then someone began beating a stick hard against the door. I heard voices shouting, "Open up!" Father jumped to open the door. When he did, a burst of steam flooded into the room. Standing in the doorway in the misty haze were two policemen. They looked strange in their blue uniforms, gold–colored buttons glittering on their chests. I watched their eyes. They had a look about them like the eyes of some animals I had seen when Father found them dead in his traps.

The policeman questioned Father in jocular, but menacing, tones. "What did you bring this time?" They used his surname with both familiarity and contempt. I could see the light from their flashlight darting here and there in the shed and in the darkness beyond.

The policemen found the knapsacks, which were packed with frozen fish and moose meat. Father had gone ice- fishing the day before in preparation for the visit to town. He left the cabin before sunup and returned late in the day with a cache of frozen fish. I remembered his face covered with ice crystals.

The policemen arrested my father for hunting and fishing out of season. They then hauled him and his knapsack off to the police station, leaving his family without any food except for the remains of the rabbit stew simmering on the back of the stove.

Father was confined in jail until court was held.

Weekly court sessions were held in the town, and Father often spent several days in jail while awaiting trial. Whenever he appeared in court, he wore the same clothes he had been dragged away in, usually a red–checkered flannel shirt and gray baggy work pants. Yet he looked tidy, and his black hair was always neatly combed.

When the judge called his name, Father stood tall and proud before him. The judge read the indictment: "Edward Paibomsai, you are charged with hunting and fishing out of season. How do you plead?" Father would not answer but reached into his shirt pocket and pulled out a well-worn piece of paper that he handed to the judge. After reading the document, the judge dismissed the charges against him

What my father had shown to the judge was that part of the Robinson Huron Treaty which read in part: "As long as the grass grows green, and the rivers flow" members of the tribe could hunt and fish without any restrictions. He, Edward Paibomsai, was a member of the tribe.

Father walked down the aisle of the courtroom looking straight at his family, who were waiting for him at the back of the courtroom. This scene was played out many times. Nothing ever changed in this drama, except for the characters and the weather.

When we did come into town unscathed, when our food supplies remained intact, Father bartered or sold some of the fresh moose meat or fish to the local townspeople. I often accompanied him as he went throughout the town and to the outlying farmhouses. I watched, sometimes in disbelief, as he interacted with the immigrant people he encountered. I heard individuals speak English in strange accents as Father negotiated with them, each trying to outdo the other, hoping for a better bargain, I supposed.

I observed the strange ways and different customs of the people

Father met. I watched a rabbi prepare meat in a slaughterhouse and asked Father, "Why does he wear a funny hat?" I ate Russian black bread, drank cold buttermilk taken from a root cellar on a Ukrainian farm, and watched in awe at Easter as a Polish neighbor painted traditional designs on eggs. For a penny a glass, I could buy homemade root beer from our English neighbor. (Father himself always sipped a glass of homemade Italian wine when it was offered to him.)

I wondered at times, when we walked the dusty sidewalks of that small town, *Who had called the police? and How had they known when we had arrived in town?*

Strangely enough, my family was occasionally invited to the community's festivities. Sometimes it was a Polish wedding or a square dance held by French– speaking hosts; at other times it was a gathering of Scots at which bagpipes were played. Father stepped out the back door to hoist a jug of "home–brew" with the men at the party. Mother square-danced to the music of the violin, guitar, and accordion. We kids watched the grownups dance then ran between the dancers and in and out of the door playing hide and seek to the strains of haunting music floating in the black night.

STORYTELLING ON WINTER NIGHTS

If Father were unexpectedly caught in a blizzard, we anxiously waited in the cabin for his safe return. A lamp sent flickering shadows around the otherwise darkened room. Terrified, we waited. Outside the cabin, powerful winds shrieked unceasingly in a tempo that tortured the soul. After waiting for what seemed like an eternity, we inevitably heard sleigh bells tinkling far off in the distance. As the sounds came closer, we could hear the dogs barking as Father's strong voice hurled out commands.

Father would always unshackle the dogs' harness and care for them before entering the cabin. When he came in, the rest of us could gage the severity of the storm by looking at him. Snow usually covered him, and crystal icicles hung from the rabbit fur that partially covered his face. Peering out from behind them, his eyes were bright with excitement. In his hand he carried the catch of the day, which he would present to Mother with a flourish: "We can have partridge stew tonight." Mother then stoked the fire and put water to boil. She asked us kids to peel potatoes, while she deftly plucked and cleaned the thawed-out bird for cooking.

We all laughed and talked as we ate our late evening meal. If Father were in one of his story-telling moods he would regale us kids with stories of his boyhood. He told about what it was like growing up on the reserve in southern Ontario, and how the people of the reserve patiently waited in the spring to tap maple trees. With glee he recalled how his father poured maple syrup on snow to make maple sugar candy for his children. We kids listened in disbelief. We scoffed at him. To make candy from trees was too far-fetched we thought. All we did in the northern tundra was to pick bitter-tasting rosin from trees to chew as gum.

The story of how maple sugar was discovered has been handed down in oral tradition for centuries. Recently, the youth of the Whitefish First Nation Reserve have preserved it in writing: It is said that a lazy Ojibway wife who liked to go visiting added maple sap to her rabbit stew because she did not want to run to the river to get water. Then she left the pot simmering on the coals of the fire while she went visiting. Returning several hours later, she found chunks of maple sugar in the pot.

SPRING IN THE NORTH COUNTRY

When spring came to the north country the warm winds from the south flowed and the tempo of the earth quickened. The days lengthened. The spring sun shone with a brilliance totally unlike the dullness of the winter sun. The intensity of the sun's rays pierced the lake and melted the ice, cracking it open with thunderous noise. The snows melted and ran in speeding rivulets to swell the waters of the lake.

My family's pace of life quickened too, as our lives were controlled by the seasonal changes. In the winter we lived in the cabin as if in a cocoon, just like the hibernating animals around us. Father kept on with his tasks of ice-fishing and hunting, but the rest of us rarely ventured out with him.

In the spring it was a time for our family to shed our winter life and to prepare for the summer ahead. We overhauled the cabin, washing and scrubbing it clean. Father oiled his traps and stored his snowshoes and toboggans. He melted down gunshot pellets to make bullets for his rifle, rendering one of our scarce pots useless. A fire burned outside the cabin, its blue smoke wafting up and disappearing into tall pine trees. Mother made soap, using fat she had saved during the winter months. She added lye to it, and let it cool in a black iron pot. When it hardened she cut it into fat, square chunks which we used to wash clothes. Sometimes, when we ran out of face soap, we used it for washing ourselves as well.

Visitors rarely came, but when they did it was usually in the spring. A French trapper or an Indian on his way to the lumber camp across the lake might stop briefly to visit. The men sat on the stoop of the cabin in the warmth of the spring day. They shared information about where the best place was to portage on a particular lake or river. They drew maps on the ground with sticks, then stamped on them and filed the knowledge away to memory.

THE LUMBER CAMP COOK

At that time of year, we also crossed the lake to the lumber camp, bringing fresh fish and game to barter with the cook for basic supplies. Father woke us early on the day we were to go. After a quick breakfast of cold bannock and hot sweet tea, we rushed out of the cabin, ran down to the dock, jumped into the canoe, and paddled vigorously through the gray mist that covered the lake.

We approached the lumber camp to find the cook leaning against the door of the cookhouse while he smoked. When he saw my father, he threw his cigarette on the ground and stepped forward to shake hands. The cook's apron was gray and grimy. His head of scraggly hair was tied with a red kerchief.

Father and he proceeded to negotiate. I often wondered why they went through this charade. The cook was French and spoke English with a strong accent. During the discussion he threw in Indian and French words and gestured wildly with his hands and arms. Father stood passively before him and interjected only a few words. The two men finally came to some agreement: perhaps a slab of salt pork for the fish, or the hindquarter of a deer for sugar, tea and flour.

After the deal was made the cook invited us into the cookhouse for lunch. That invitation was what we kids had been looking forward to when we crossed the lake. The cookhouse was an exciting place to visit. It differed greatly from our cabin, which was cluttered with snowshoes, traps, and animal furs on stretchers. Our food was stored in a small space beside the stove, and our plates and cups were made of tin. The cook's kitchen, however, had shelves on the wall filled with shiny containers. A wood barrel with bulging sides stood on the floor, and a spice shelf hung beside the big, black stove. The rough-hewn pine table and floors were scrubbed clean, and the odor of strong soap still clung to them. Fruit pies cooled alongside loaves of brown, crusted bread. The smell of cinnamon and cloves scented the room.

The cook offered us sandwiches; canned corn beef on thick slices of home-made bread. Later we munched huge slices of dried apple pie, and drank hot tea with canned milk that was served to us in white enamel cups. I held the cup with my finger and looked at Father. "Look Papa, they have handles on them." He smiled.

Mayflowers In The Spring

Father shook his children awake saying, "Wake up. Hurry! We are going to see the mayflowers today. Get dressed." Quietly moving around in the cabin so as not to wake Mother, we packed a lunch of cold bannock and molasses, and left the cabin just as dawn was breaking.

Some spattering of snow remained on the ground. We walked miles through the tangled brush and muskeg, laughing and chattering like the chipmunks and birds around us. Stopping to rest, we quieted down and listened to the sounds of the earth, to an absolute rhythm of silence. When we started to walk again in pursuit of the elusive flowers, we hollered out to Father who was barging on ahead of us: "How far are we going? Where are we going?"

He never answered us but kept right on going, pushing the brush away and looking to right and left. Most likely he had seen the flowers when he was out hunting but now he was not quite sure where. Finally he stopped short, gathered his children around him and pointed to the ground in front of him. In an excited voice, he said, "Look, here they are! Don't pick them. Just look at them. "We looked to where he was pointing. A cluster of creamy white, waxlike petals nestled on shiny jade-colored leaves spread on lime-colored moss. They had burst to new spring life on the grayish black rocks that were molded to the cold hard ground. We leaned down to get a closer look.

This was the art—the *museum*—that Father had taken time to show his children.

We started back, walking quietly at first, but soon our youthful exuberance returned. Mother, as usual, was back at home, doing her woman's work.

Leaving the North Country

The war effort in Canada during the Second World War caused a massive shift in Canada's demographics as people migrated to the cities to work in major industries. I, too, left the northern wilderness and my family at that time and traveled to a city in southern Ontario. I was eighteen in 1944, and despite my lack of either an education or work experience, I soon found a job in a small café in the inner city. There I met a man. We married and moved to Boston, Massachusetts.

Shortly after I arrived in the United States in 1948 my mother died. Since my two older sisters had left for the spirit world when they were in their twenties, my father and I were the only surviving members of our immediate family. But that same year (1948) I lost contact with my father. Unbeknownst to me, he had returned to his reserve, a fact I remained unaware of for thirty years. (I now know we lost contact because neither of us knew how to have our home address changed at the local post office.) I regret that I never heard from my father again, but it is how it came to be that I found myself adrift in a strange city without family or tribal affiliations.

I was out of contact with all I had ever known and all that I was familiar with. I was overwhelmed by the assimilation process. In the years that followed I bore three children. Each pregnancy was difficult with serious complications (toxemia) setting in. I was left with hypertension. When life's troubles came to me I was literally without a place to return to. I had been raised in the wilderness of Canada, where I was deprived of the benefit of reserve or communal life, and in a small town, where I had been exposed to racial injustice.

My first experience of the havoc of city life occurred when I became a victim of spousal abuse. When I contacted a social agency for assistance I was firmly and rudely awakened to the fact that I was totally alone and without a support system. The social workers turned down my plea for help, a decision that was based mainly on my husband's work record. He was a city employee who supported his family, whereas I had been arrested for drunkenness. Once. Since I was found to be at fault I was compelled to stay in the marriage and to endure six years of abuse before I found a way to leave my husband and the marriage.

Every Friday night my husband got drunk at the neighborhood bar. He came home at midnight and roused me out of sleep by yanking at my hair and throwing me to the floor. These attacks continued several times before I finally figured out how to avoid them. Thereafter, every Friday night just before midnight, I gathered up a few pillows and placed them in the bathtub to make a bed for myself. As I lay in the tub reading, I thought how unreal the situation was. I felt most keenly the deprivation of love that his actions caused me and the children.

I had never seen or experienced abusiveness when I was a child. It was not a reality in my parents' lives. I have since thought deeply about why I have experienced marriages that were disruptive but have come up with a zero explanation.

I never accepted the conditions in my marriage but somehow remained detached and passive throughout the experience. I thought there was no way out. Eventually, after four years of binge drinking, I found a self-help group; and then later I found a way out of the marriage.

Recovering alcoholics make strange friendships. A person in the self-help group I attended gave me professional references. With them in hand, I applied for and was hired as a live-in maid in a middle-class suburb of Boston. Finally, after many years of living in a bad situation, I was able to think and make a move to get out of it. I made arrangements for the children to be cared for in a family group home, and I left the apartment and my husband. It was three months before my husband decided he would leave the apartment. That was when I returned to it with my children.

I soon discovered I was not fulfilling my role as a single parent as well as I ought. I was on Aid to Dependent Children but did not know how to manage the small amount of money I received. Shortly after I was divorced, my children and I were evicted from our housing project apartment. I hadn't paid the rent. When I was in my twenties I had been diagnosed with hypertension, and many of the decisions I later made were based on that condition. I sought out a family counselor at this time and remained in therapy with her for twelve years. The counselor ably assisted me with the children's needs. She even made arrangements for them to attended camp each summer.

After several years of therapeutic counseling, the counselor evaluated my progress. She felt I was not improving as well as I should (the assimilation process and the years of being a battered wife had taken its toll). She suggested and arranged for the two youngest children to be sent from the home. My son, age twelve, went to a preparatory school, and my eight-year-old daughter was placed in a foster home. When she was twelve, she too was enrolled in private school.

Throughout those years I lived with fear. Eventually, I read about "fight or flight" syndrome, which described accurately how I felt. I was terrorized so much that I literally was unable to speak in the self-help group I attended for twenty years.

It is difficult to bring back and write about the memories of that painful time but those years did pass. The children grew up. My oldest daughter was sixteen when she left home and went to New York, where she abused drugs. It was ten years before I saw her again. I had several operations. My younger daughter came home weekends from her school. Although my son visited his father on weekends, I saw him frequently. I received new medicine for my hypertension, and the illness I suffered from became manageable.

I also remarried. My second husband was diagnosed a maniac depressive. By this time I had been in a self-help group for ten years. Despite its positive philosophy, I remained extremely dependent on my husband. We lived in the Back Bay of Boston. Periodically, he suffered from depression and underwent treatment at a veteran's hospital.

In my second marriage I spent hours at a bridge table. I sanded and varnished a sailboat at a local marina and sailed in Boston Harbor. I attended art classes. I became a gourmet cook. I was always an avid reader, and I now read compulsively. For the first time in my life I had unlimited access to books. The first magazines and paperback books I found when I came to the city were in the used book stores. I soon discovered the public library and read many books, including the classics.

Although my children were brought up away from me, we remained close—that is until their later teenage years. I looked forward to their visits and enjoyed our time together when they returned to the city on weekends. I anticipated and planned special dinners for them. We celebrated holidays together. They went iceskating on Boston Common, and we spent hours together before they returned to their respective schools.

I never learned how to balance a checkbook, never learned how to drive a car. I lapsed into silences that lasted a day or two. I was divorced again.

I went job hunting whenever I felt able to work, and was to eventually work first as a domestic day-worker and later as a banquet waitress.

I learned how to cut my own hair since the barbers or hair stylists did not want me as client. They told me so. Henri, a hair stylist on Newbury Street said if I were seen in his salon, it would send his customers away. Henri is long-since gone. (Did he pass on his racial views to his children? I suppose so, as that is how values are handed down from one generation to the next.)

What I felt most keenly in the transition from one social environment to another was the loss of family and a familiar environment: the cold climate; the snow; the blizzards; the fishing; and the hunting. I missed Nature: the earth, the trees, the rippling water in the lakes and river. The city, void of these elements, was barren and cold. Cement walks and high canyon walls of bricks always surrounded me. The walls of my housing project were sky high. The noises of the city—trucks, fire engines, ambulances—shrieked unceasingly. I walked on sidewalks that glittered in the summer rain. The wild winds of a nor'easter in New England blasted snow on the city streets, a familiarly nostalgic event.

But I was not to return to the land or my birth for the next forty years (there was no one there for me.) My children were away at school. This was the reality or fate I created and lived with that remained unchanged for many years.

Back Bay

In October 1972 I buried my son. Standing beside me that bright autumn day were young men, the "Vietnam Veterans Against the War." They had come in a gesture of support to say farewell to a fallen comrade. With their long hair and bearded, unshaven faces, they looked shaggy and unkempt in their old army jackets. Their expressions were grim and their eyes burned with a passion that spoke of where they had been and what they had seen. I am eternally grateful for their gesture. The casket lay on the ground covered with the red, white and blue of the American flag. The fall air was clear, the winds brisk. I looked to the sky. I held my breath tight. I caught a glimpse of clouds breaking up and like a puff of smoke vanished into the white air.

"I will be decorated like a Christmas tree when I come home, Ma. I have the bronze star. The purple heart. The Vietnam medal of honor." The image of that day stayed with me through the long bleak years that followed.

That same year, when I was forty-eight years old, my life's journey took other turns: my marriage of ten years dissolved; and my younger daughter married. (My older daughter had left home ten years earlier.)

That was also the year I moved to a studio apartment in Boston's Back Bay. The room was large and elegantly furnished. A petite rosewood desk and chair were positioned by a window overlooking a courtyard. A grand oriental rug covered the hardwood floor. A mahogany bureau, along with other American furniture reminiscent of the early 1900s, completed the decor.

In the back courtyard a single tree stood beside the brick wall.

During the first six months I spent in my new environment, my mind wandered and went spinning out of control. I fell into a clinical depression. All I could seemingly do at that point was to sit robot-like before a television, chain smoking and drinking huge amounts of coffee. I lost weight as I could not stand in line in the supermarkets to buy food. When I did make the attempt to do so, I panicked and fled from the store as if the hounds of hell were chasing me.

A part of me shut down. I existed in some kind of vacuum. I was to became a loner, and it was there in that room that I lived a life of isolation for the next ten years. I could barely function in the workplace or in the various action groups I later attended. I was unable to focus what energy I had to help me directly; instead, I remained only vaguely aware of things around me. I wondered if I was ever going to come to terms with the reality of being alone. I knew with a just certainty that my roles of mother and wife were forever over. *What would I do? What could I do? Was I going make it through?*

In previous years I had worked sporadically in the food industry. Since I was now without financial support, I went looking for such a job again. But I could not find one. I felt it was because of my age, and that conclusion led me to believe that I was too old to work in any fast-paced industry. After analyzing the situation as best I could, I decided to enroll in a typing program. At a desk by a window, I practiced on an old typewriter—an antique I got from God-knows-where. Tears without crying fell down my face.

I looked out the window to see the leaves on the trees motionless in the hot summer air.

Somewhere I heard or read about sublimated activities. I began to write depressing poetry and brought oil paints back to the room and attempted to paint. These were futile gestures. Wild with rage, I threw the paint boards to the floor and stomped on them.

It was a tremendous effort to pull myself together whenever I met with my young married daughter. Thankfully, her youthful husband and friends were devoted to her and supported her during this trying time.

I made various attempts to pull myself out of the psychological shock I was in, but when I did, it was just for brief periods. I always fell back. I wondered if I was ever going to face up to the challenges of a new day. How do you go about rethinking your thoughts? Old grooves run deep. How can new information and concepts be processed while you are in an agitated state? The questions went on and on. I was finding change to be difficult in so-called normal times.

I had no strength to do daily routines, let alone remake an entire life. In the past I had found it difficult to adapt to change, and I just knew I hadn't been successful in anything I had ever done. Except, perhaps, survive.

Six months later, when I was well enough, I attended several the meetings of several activist groups in the Boston area: Gold Star Mothers Against the War, a strongly feminist organization based in Cambridge, and the American Indian Movement. I always sat quietly in the back of the hall at these meetings, never offering any comments or suggestions. The members in each group enthusiastically voiced their concerns with rhetoric that was totally unfamiliar to me. I soon learned, however, to mimic the various phrases I heard. In one group I attended I learned to swear like a seasoned trooper. In another I wore the garb of the militant Indian: blue jeans, blue denim jacket, and a red shirt. I was not able to communicate well with anyone on a friendly basis, but during my drinking sprees (which occurred every two or three months) I reversed this trend. I became a "motor mouth" and discussed with clarity the issues espoused by those groups with anyone who would listen, even with strangers I met at a neighborhood bar.

I stood alone by the window and watched large snowflakes fall slowly and gracefully to the ground.

My life was becoming full and vital again. I was working full-time, and my first grandchild was born. I was still in recovery, however, when, four years later, life struck me yet another blow.

My oldest daughter returned to Boston broken in health. Despite her condition (cirrhosis) and the years of drug abuse, she retained an enthusiastic spirit of life. She loved the pageantry of Christmas—indeed, the entire winter season. She had a flair for style and enjoyed coordinating her clothes. But soon after she returned to Boston, she was murdered.

After this second horrendous passage in my life, I went into a world without light. I walked the streets of the city with my head down. My heart and spirit were crushed with pain. I lived with an enormous sense of guilt. I thought to myself: *If only I had been a better mother; If only I had an education.* These thoughts haunted me. If only I had known what to do, if only I had known how to live in this society, I might have had more control over my life and destiny. The bleakness of my life returned and remained with me for eight more years.

In September, the fall winds screeched unceasingly as they rushed through the deserted alley. I looked out the window to see the branches of the tree stripped of leaves. They were bare and shook hideously in the wind.

I reflected constantly on past memories. I probed and analyzed a particular incident over and over again. I looked for an explanation for why I led such a disastrous life. I desperately needed to know. This obsessive and insidious process kept my mind racing. Regret and remorse over the choices I had made in my life filled my whole being. I thought, *If only I had chosen one incident over the other. I was pushing one slot into another.* I had to do it. I had to make it fit. It was an exhausting process and left me depleted of energy.

My abuse of alcohol aggravated and prolonged this condition. I was in my middle fifties when a glimmering of rationality entered my mind, and I began to make serious attempts to stop my obsessive negative thinking. I reasoned that if I could find a way to stop this obsession, I would make the attempt to get on with whatever was left of my life. After this positive thought entered the bleak maze of my consciousness (the result of ten years of negative thinking), I decided I must take immediate action if I were ever going to climb out of my black hole of depression. I was at a point in my life when conditions could seriously improve or seriously worsen.

I began the healing process by looking at my past. I had a definite goal in mind: I would write about it, or at least *attempt* to do so. I thought about how old I was but did not consider my age to be a handicap. I threw away the traditional concepts of aging (or perhaps didn't know any better) and went off to pursue an academic career. I knew I would continue to work through the various preconceptions of the phase I was in. I felt grief—painful grief—as I moved slowly into another time, into to the new flow of events that was to take place in my life.

I looked out the window to see that the tree's lime-green buds had burst open. The tree was in full bloom. It looked magnificent standing alone against the brick courtyard in the alley.

The Boston Indian Council

In the late 1960s the Indians of Canada and the United States stopped being quiescent and began confronting their governments with demands to be included in the vast social changes sweeping their countries. They asked for representation in the decision–making process and for the right of self–government on their reserves and reservations, concepts not recognized in the Indian policies of Canada or the United States.

This renascence for Native people began and gathered momentum after Indian activists organized the takeover of the abandoned federal prison on Alcatraz Island in San Francisco Bay in 1969. At roughly the same time, other Indians, mainly Ojibways in Minneapolis and St. Paul organized the American Indian Movement (AIM). Soon, AIM members included urban and reservation Indians from tribes across the United States and Canada. Actions taken by these young Indians inspired and raised the spirits of Indian people across the United States and Canada. Not since the days of Crazy Horse, the Sioux chief, had the Indian Nation felt such a sense of exhilaration. As a feeling of liberation swept over Indian Country, Indian people began the monumental effort of organizing themselves in the cities and on the reservations.

In the late sixties a group of Micmac teenagers migrated to Boston from their reserves in Canada. They arrived in the city without work experience, skills, or an education. They also had no support system in place to assist them in the transition from reservation life to survival in the city. They soon found a haven, however, in a drop–in center for alcoholics located in Boston's skid-row. They also gathered at a small park in the same section of the city. Soon it became known as "Indian Park," where Indians living in Boston and Native American students from Harvard University's Indian Program began to meet and discuss contemporary Indian issues.

Shortly after these meetings began, members organized and drafted a charter for a non-profit organization. The Boston Indian Council (B.I.C.) opened in 1972, a multi–service center to serve Indian people living in Boston and elsewhere in New England.

The organization eventually moved into a four–story brick

building in the Jamaica Plain area of Boston that had been designed and constructed in the early twenties to house juvenile delinquents. Cells, small six-by-twelve rooms with barred openings in the door, lined the corridors of the first and second floor. (The cells were later used as offices.) A gym was centered on the first floor.

On the day of the opening, a bus came to a gradual stop in front of the building. The bus door opened, and Dana Jones jumped lightly out and walked casually into the center. He was a lithe, winsome-looking fellow. He wore blue jeans and a denim jacket, and a red bandanna circled his black hair. He had flung his medicine bag jauntily over his shoulder.

Dana was a shaman who, at the request of the center, had come from the Black Hills of South Dakota to conduct the spiritual ceremonies on opening day.

Community members and employees of the organization gathered to celebrate the opening. Some people standing in the circle in the gym that day had long-ceased practicing their tribal rituals because of lack of community. Now, they waited in silence as the shaman prepared the braids of sweet grass. Fragrant smoke rose from the vessel and filtered through the hall. The shaman smudged the people, who brought the smoke to themselves in sweeping gestures. They then traipsed behind Dana as he went about the building to cleanse each room with smoke.

The festivities continued throughout the day. Piles of food filled the tables in the gym. After feasting on buffalo stew and wild rice, singers gathered around the drum and raised their voices in song.

The shaman spoke. He told how in the distant past the Ojibway people came from the land of roses and the blue waters that is now known as Ontario to the three hills that once stood high overlooking the waters of Boston Harbor "The hills," he said, "were spiritual ground for the Indian Nation and were called the Three Sisters, and were a mecca for Indian people who made pilgrimages from all of North America to hold ceremonial rituals there." (The hills were leveled during the development of modern Boston.)

In somber tones, the shaman continued: "The people left us a spiritual legacy to be passed down to each succeeding generation. Four hundred years have now passed since our people held the sacred pipe on the high hills; but now the descendants of the tribal people who once gathered there to perform their sacred ceremonies are here in this hall, and in celebration of our endurance to the changes that have come to our way of life, we will dance today, respectfully, on the varnished floors of this building. For our ancestors have passed this ritual down to us as we will do for the next seven generations. The tall hills of which I speak, once extended high to the sky. It was a place where the eagle and sky were closely connected, and where a power source freely flowed."

Indians from Canada and the United States joined the center's workforce. They were as strangers meeting for the fist time, for they came from various geographic locations and practiced different tribal customs. However, they soon discovered that they shared a common denominator: an invisible bond of rawhide held them close in a tradition and culture that has existed since time began.

I worked at the Indian multi-service center from 1972 to 1985, during which time I attended conferences and workshops on Native American Indian issues. In 1975 a mandate of a federally funded program suggested employees take college courses relating to their jobs. I complied, went to a junior college and registered, even though I had only a third grade education. I was stunned when I found myself enrolled in a junior college math course. What I knew about math was how to add and subtract. I enrolled four times in the basic math course before I completed and earned a passing grade. I dropped out or took an incomplete whenever I got discouraged. I did this for a year-and-a-half. I still don't know why I persevered to do what I did, but I did! I attended three other courses that year, but except for the math course I did not enroll in any other college course the next year.

Going to College

Six years later, in 1979, I was visiting a co-worker's office when I casually mentioned that I would like to take more college courses. Coincidentally, she had met some New England educators at a task-force meeting the day before. She immediately picked up the phone and called the dean of a prestigious evening school. Then she made an appointment for me to meet with him to discuss my application for evening school. Thus it was that in mid-life I began the journey into my elder years in an outrageous fashion: I was entering the unknown (to me) world of academia. I enrolled in a prestigious New England college where for the next seven years I pursued a bachelor of arts degree.

In September 1980, I walked up a long steep hill in Newton, Massachusetts. The day was sunny and bright, the air crisp and cold—typical New England weather. I took my time. Halfway up

the hill I stopped to rest, to take short quick breaths before I continued on. Finally I reached the top of the hill in a somewhat
bedraggled condition. I looked around the campus grounds and just
knew I was out of my natural element. The size and complexity of
the buildings baffled me. They were spread out all over the place.
After I regained my composure, I asked a passing student," Where is
the Evening School?" He pointed out the direction in which I
should head, and I went on to find the building I was seeking.

Waiting in a office for the interview, I thought about what I
could say to convince the person that I was to see that I was serious
about my application. The door to a office opened and a man wearing a black checkered shirt came out. He was smiling as he greeted
me and invited me into his office. I took the seat he offered me and
looked across the desk at him. He was a big, robust man. Irish, and
a Jesuit priest! I was a short, stocky, middle-aged Indian woman with
myopic eyes hidden behind thick, tinted glasses. I was neat and tidy,
but my clothes were shabby. They had been picked from used
clothes bags donated to the center.

I answered his questions in short terse sentences. I couldn't be
free and easy with him—I just couldn't. I had just begun the climb
out of the black hole of depression I had been in for ten years. I
thought to myself, *If he really knew me,* and all the negative images
of my past, including the episodic drinking binges, rolled out before
me. Just that summer I had slept on a street bench in the south end
of Boston.

I thought he might reject me. He looked at my school records
(four courses at the community college) and talked briefly to me
about my work at the Center. Then he casually informed me that
I was accepted into the evening school and suggested I register for
classes that day. He gave me directions to the registrar's office,
and I again went out into the huge complex to search out yet
another building! Another ordeal! But a young student in the registrar's office noticed my confusion and helped me fill out the
necessary forms.

When I finished the business at hand, I walked out of the
building in a daze and down a short street. I was acutely aware of
the tall trees lining the street and noticed how they stood in pre-
cise positions alongside the path. My heart quickened. My heart
beat. I found it hard to believe that I had actually been accepted,
that I was going to attend this school. I was overcome at how easily it had been accomplished. I thought, *Wow! Oh, my God, what*

should I do, now that I will be part of this great institution?

I literally flew down the hill to the subway station. The flaming, riotous color of autumn leaves flashed a song of a new season to come. I wanted to shout with joy as I climbed the train that would take me back to the city. I wanted to celebrate, to share my joy with someone, but, being a loner as I had been and living in isolation for those many years, I had made no friends.

When I reached home, I filled a Pyrex container with water and turned on the gas stove. I made coffee, got out my favorite coffee mug, and sat down. I lit a cigarette and said, "Well, damn it, what do I do now?"

Halfway through my studies, I asked myself questions as I walked up the hill in the rain and cold bitter snows of winter or in the hot steamy weather of summer. *Why am I doing this? Why do I need a degree? I am in my fifties and have worked without a degree in my community for many years.*

I have always been an avid reader. After I learned to read (when I was seven or thereabouts) reading captured my attention. But reading material was scarce when I was a child. I read labels on cans whenever my family got them (cans were scarce as well). I read old newspapers, even when they were faded and brown, whenever I came across them. A neighbor lent me "English newspapers" containing "rags-to-riches" short stories. I was twelve when I painstakingly plodded through a well-worn Bible I found somewhere. Of course, when I was in my teens I read my share of *True Confession* magazines

At the Catholic college I attended, I was required to take two courses in theology. In one course I was required to keep a journal and write about a spiritual experience. I knew I could keep a journal, but to write about a spiritual experience was an idea I had never considered. What could I write about? I was puzzled and reasoned I had lived for the most part a traditional Indian life.

When I was a child I was exposed to the teachings of the Episcopalian church. My family attended church services occasionally when we were in town. It was something to do, just as we attended the gospel tent revival services when they were in town.

I worried how I was going to get the assignment done until I realized I've had a spiritual life in living close to nature with my family. I could and would write about how my parents related to the environment in which they lived. How they respected and honored Mother Earth and all living creatures. How they lived in harmony and adapted to the four seasons with vigorous energy and seasonal rites. How in the spring they offered the bones of the animals to the great spirit *Kitchie Manitou*. How my parents offered a daily prayer of thanksgiving to the Great Spirit for the blessings of food and shelter. This is what I could document as a spiritual experience.

Seemingly, the reflections I was obsessed with in the last five years fit the schedule I was now in, for during this period I had jotted down notes about early childhood memories.

Once I chose and started my new career, I did not plunge straight ahead and stay directly on the path. One year I dropped out of school halfway through a semester because the law course I was taking reminded me that just the year before I had been in a courtroom at the trial of my daughter's murderer. In another class the discussion was on death and dying. I fell out of my seat.

Both times I quit classes halfway through and went traveling "Indian-style" throughout America. Perhaps I should explain that term. I rationalized and justified what I was about to do before I went off to get a one-way bus fare to whatever destination I chose—perhaps it was Tucson, San Francisco, Seattle, Denver. Since I had experience in dealing with my Indian brothers and sisters who traveled this way, I knew what to do when I arrived in a strange city. No one questioned this middle-aged woman's actions, why I was traveling across the country this way. Rather, they accepted me in each Indian center I went to for assistance, and I usually found work the first week in my new environment. I returned to New England three months later and resumed classes.

Going to classes and getting a college degree wasn't an easy task. In fact, it was a real effort. Some of the classes I took were baffling to me. In a philosophy class the professor said the discussion would be about the "youths in Asia." I could not help but think, What about them? Then I discovered the subject under discussion was euthanasia!

In one literature class the professor discussed a writer's imagery of the forest as being wild and fearful. Utter nonsense, I thought. My idea of a forest was one of a deep silence of nothing with radiant yellow sunlight shining through tall, green, fresh pine trees; or perhaps it was walking through a stretch of muskeg in raw brush country where the whiplash of the trees alerted you to the presence of your companions. There was nothing fearful or wild about the wonderful air. Or in the smoky twilight of sounds and feeling of nature.

Writing of My Heritage

After years of obsessively thinking about past memories and analyzing them to the nth degree, I began writing in the 1970s.

I realized when I was in my late forties that I had little knowledge about the Ojibway tribe or my grandparents' ancestral past. How this realization came about was when my daughter began questioning her Indian background. It was in 1973 that she began to ask about the tribe and the reservation where her grandparents had been registered. Although I wasn't able to answer all her queries, I could tell her that her grandfather had come from the Whitefish River Reserve in southern Ontario and that my family received "treaty money" from this reserve on a semi-annual basis while I was growing up. I told her that her grandmother was a northern Ojibway, a "bush country Indian" just as I had been. My daughter was not entirely satisfied with the answers I gave her. Wanting more information, she called the reservation and was fortunate to locate relatives who invited her to visit them.

The Whitefish First Nation Reserve—the tribe I am identified with—is located 500 miles northeast of Toronto. In 1978 my daughter and I journeyed to the land where Father had been born, to the reserve I heard about in his storytelling days. Because I was grieving the loss of my son, and had only recently divorced, I barely recall any details about the reserve or about the meeting with my relatives. I do, however, remember climbing a steep hill and seeing Cradle Rock, a large, hollowed-out stone where shamans had sought vision quests in the Ojibways' distant past. I was transfixed with awe as I stood alongside it. It was as if the spirits of the past were present and the power of the medicine men were reaching out to me as I stood silently, giving homage to them. One of those medicine men, I knew, had been a Paibomsai.

My father's relatives assured me that I was a welcome addition to the family and to the tribe, saying to me, "We did not know you existed." Still, I did not appreciate the significance of being on Father's reserve and meeting relatives I had only heard about in his stories.

After I returned from Canada I continued to live a life of isolation for the next seven years and did not pursue any additional information about my tribe or family members. In 1978 I began my studies at Boston College. To fulfill a course requirement I submitted a paper on my parents..

In 1987 I entered the Urban Fellowship Program at the

Massachusetts Institute of Technology (M.I.T.) in Cambridge, Massachusetts. During that year I accomplished several goals: I traveled to Toronto to research the Ojibway tribe and my own family's background; I completed a computer search for material about Native American women of the Northeast and discovered a scarcity of available literature; and I interviewed a Micmac woman and wrote a brief sketch about her life. I also began to think about writing about the assimilation process that I had personally experienced. I took the initial steps to do just that—never realizing that seven years later I would be still working on it! I completed my studies that year by submitting a children' story.

I recalled the events that took place prior to making my decision to make the journey to Toronto in the winter of 1987-88. I was an Urban Community Fellow at Massachusetts Institute of Technology (M.I.T.) that year, and it was during the fall semester that year I had researched the available literature on Native American women of the East Coast, finding a scarcity of material, little, if any, of it produced by Native women themselves. With that in mind, I began the journey to research my own ancestry and the history of the Ojibway Nation.

I was sixty–three, an age when society considers you "over the hill," and I was also without research funds. During the academic year 1987-99, while at M.I.T., I submitted a proposal for funding to carry on my work, but the granting agency turned me down. Naturally, I was disappointed when I received the notice of rejection, and I reacted by thinking only negative thoughts. My head became a mecca of self–pity and anger, emotions that simply plied my soul until, "*WOW,* " I remembered my survival skills!

Still, negative thoughts continued, until the idea of positive thinking slid into my consciousness and shrugged off whatever was left of the anger. I decided to move on, to go on regardless, as I had a strong feeling about my project and what I would be able to document. Furthermore, I would be writing from an Indian *woman's* perspective of what it was like to migrate from one society to another. I would continue to work, despite the lack of support, except of course the Indian community center in Toronto.

I called the Toronto center immediately. I needed their assistance. I needed someone, anyone, if I was to continue: the material I needed to research was housed in the Provincial Parliament buildings in Toronto.

When I spoke to the director of the Women's Resource Center in Toronto and gave her the information she requested, I asked, "Would I fit the criteria they needed to have me as one of their guests." She called me back later that week to tell me that I could indeed spend some time in their residence. I had explained that I would be without funds when I arrived. In fact, I would be destitute. But I was an elder, a woman, and an Ojibway.

As I boarded the plane in Boston, I had mixed feelings about embarking on this journey. *Did I have the necessary confidence? How would I accomplish the tasks before me? Was I physically capable of doing them?* I was age sixty-three when I began the project and had some misgivings about age and its related mythical elements. I had not been back in Canada, the land of my birth, but twice in forty years. I had no reason to return; my family had long since gone.

I arrived in Toronto in the winter of 1988. Snow was on the ground and the air was bitterly cold. I rode the airport bus into the city; once there, I hailed a taxi to take me to my destination. Later on, after been driven around much of downtown Toronto by an amiable taxi driver, I finally arrived at the center.

Indian groups in Toronto established the transition house in 1970 to provide food and shelter for native women who were making the transition to urban life. The house did not discriminate against other racial groups but included women from all cultures. The philosophy of the house was to help *women* in need.

I was assigned the task of cleaning the laundry room early each morning. When I finished I left the house each day armed with information to master the city's complex subway system and how to locate the government buildings. As I walked through the stately halls and the expansive marbled floors of the official buildings, I felt as insignificant as a mouse scurrying around a large floor. I felt overwhelmed by the impressive grandeur. I carried a gray cloth bag over my shoulder filled with the usual equipment researchers carry: pen, notebook, camera, and tape recorder.

As I walked along, I would think to myself, *What the hell are you doing? What exactly are you trying to prove, you old fool?* In some ways it had the sense of the ridiculous.

To rid myself of this negativism, I tried to think of a challenging thought. I wondered, *What will I name this document?* I could not think and gave up. Then I remembered that I was in the land of my birth. I was in Canada! I was a Canadian! That thought was overpowering.

My first official stop was at the Northern Indian Affairs offices. The gentleman behind the information desk greeted me cordially. He responded to my questions about the Ojibway tribe by giving me a handbook on existing treaties between the Ojibway tribes and the Canadian government. I leafed through the handbook and was amazed when I came across a familiar name: Paibomsai. My own Indian name!

I had contacted the Whitefish River Reserve band office prior to leaving home to ask their permission to come to the reserve to research my family name and the Ojibway tribe. I was informed that I would have to send a letter of intent to the Band Council, which would take up my request at its next meeting. Although I had only limited knowledge of my father's background, I did know he had belonged to this particular reserve and I knew that I had been registered there at birth as well. My family had received treaty money from this particular tribe on a semi-annual basis—sometimes the only money we saw in a given year. If we were in the bush country at treaty money time, we made a trip to town to buy food supplies and basic necessities.

I spent four days in Toronto before I continued on my journey. After reading documents from the Whitefish River Reserve in the archives in Toronto, I was startled to discover that my great-grandfather had been a co-signer of the Robinson Huron treaty. It was a great moment when I realized that my ancestor was a key figure in the sequence of events that had brought change to the Ojibway people and that his involvement in the treaties of the nineteenth century was recorded for posterity.

Permission had been granted for me to come to the reserve. I called the band office a second time and asked to be put in touch with a Paibomsai. I informed them that my father Edward Paibomsai had left the reserve forty years ago, and had returned there when he was age seventy. "Do you remember him or the name?" I asked. The name, I was told, was a familiar one; if I called back later they would get me in touch with someone. That same week, I received a call from a relative who said that she would be glad to have me visit her. In going this far in tracing my family background and historical roots, I felt amazed that I had actually committed myself to this search.

When I arrived at the Whitefish River Reserve I felt more "at ease" than I had during my first trip there, probably because I had acquired more knowledge about the place and its people.

Approximately three miles wide and ten miles long, Whitefish River Reserve is located on the north shore of Georgian Bay, north of Manitoulin and midway between Sudbury (to the east) and Sault Ste. Marie (to the west). The reserve's vegetation is typical of the Great Lakes and St. Lawrence region. Dense forests of hemlock, cedar, hard maple, white birch, poplar, and ash cover the hilly terrain. Strawberries, cranberries, chokeberries, and blueberries grow wild on the reserve. Small lakes and rivers dot the landscape. The reserve's public school, church, and community center are surrounded by the ranch-style homes of the residents.

Four hundred members of the Whitefish River band of Ojibways live on the reserve itself, while another eight hundred live elsewhere. Most band members practice the Roman Catholic religion, but traditional values and customs are also in evidence. The band is an active member of the larger Anishinabe Nation and is affiliated with both the Union of Ontario Indians and the six-band tribal council called the United Chiefs and Councils of Manitoulin (U.C.C.M.).

At the reserve I met relatives and many other people at a Sunday church service, where I was introduced as a Paibomsai. I heard people say, "She looks like us." As I shook hands, some said, "We didn't know you existed.!" I remember thinking, likewise, I'm sure. I was shown a burial ground where generations of Paibomsai were buried.

When we came to the community grounds I noticed a ten-by-six-foot weathered, gray wooden building standing in the center. I was informed that it was there as a reminder of the old days. Looking at it, I had a sense of what it must have been like when my grandfather's store had been in the same building. I felt proud—really proud—that an ancestor like him was in my genealogy.

After my stay on the reserve I traveled three hundred miles north to meet with cousins who gave me further information about Mother's family tree. I examined a time-work sheet of the Hudson's Bay Company that Great-Great-Grandfather had signed in 1830.

For me, as an elder, the trip and the task of researching my tribal connections became an exciting adventure as I continued exploring the trails my ancestors had taken seven generations past.

The same year that I visited the reserve I went to Ottawa and visited its Indian Center. While there, I also demonstrated outside the Parliament Buildings with Cree Indians who had come from their isolated community three hundred miles north of the capital.

They were concerned with toxic waste that was being dumped into a lake they used for drinking and cooking water.

In 1987 I graduated from Boston College with a Bachelor of Arts degree in social science. Several years later I submitted an application to Mel King, Director of the Urban Community Fellowship Program at the Massachusetts Institute of Technology. I was accepted into the program. While at M.I.T. as a Community Fellow, I embarked on several projects. One was to research my ancestry and the history of the Ojibway tribe, of which I am a member. That same year I interviewed Rita (whose story is in this book) and became acutely aware that information about Native American women—particularly those of the Northeast—was scarce and hard to locate.

Although I began to document the autobiographies of Native American women ten years ago, I did not write on a daily basis. Rather, I have lived my elder years involved in many different projects and rewarding experiences. Since receiving my degree from Boston College I have enrolled in several writing courses at Radcliffe Seminars Cambridge. One semester I even took a course in watercolors. I spent that semester concentrating on sketching and painting feathers. I have been a "Sunday painter" for several years now. During the eight weeks I attended the class, I sketched with watercolors and colored pencils. Along with other mature members of the class, I sat on the floor in the halls of museums sketching birds and animals. It was a break from the ordinary. (I would like to use the word "mundane", but nothing in my life has ever been "mundane!")

Four years ago I directed and produced a video, *Wampanoag Women Speak*, which was shown on local television stations and is now on file in the library of the Native American Indian Program at Harvard University. I have also lectured at various New England colleges and have written two children's books; although they both remain unpublished, one was accepted as my "body of work" for the M.I.T. Fellowship Program.

My most enriching experience, however, has simply been being a grandmother to my four grandchildren.

Today I live in a high-rise apartment in downtown Boston but eagerly leave it on weekends during the summer to follow the pow-wow trail, selling Native American jewelry. Most powwows take place in rural New England. In the countryside I feel close to nature and to the power of the earth. I arrive at the powwow grounds early, when the sun is just coming up over the trees. The field is quiet, the grass is wet, and leaves rustle in the wind. Across the field comes the sound of a flute playing, its high notes drifting hauntingly in the air.

In the city I occasionally look out my window to watch the full moon rise alongside a concrete building. In the summer, the water in a reflecting pool shows the sky in the church in the churchyard across the street. I walk through city parks with a pensive step and observe the neatly landscaped grass and behold the sight of colorful flowers growing in uniform spaces. Thus, when I leave my urban environment in the spring to venture out into the countryside to vend my jewelry until early fall, I feel close to the earth—whether the days be the hot, humid ones of summer or the cold, damp, and rainy ones of fall.

2 ⬡

Anne's Story

The Micmac reserves in Canada are located in the provinces of Nova Scotia, Newfoundland, and Quebec. Like the other 300-plus indigenous tribes of North America, the Micmacs had their own political and social systems before the Europeans invaded their homeland. The values behind these systems were taught by example.

In Micmac country it is believed that the rules governing their lives had been set up by the Creator. It is vital that each Micmac learn and accept these rules, presented to them as a gift from the Creator.

Micmac traditions were presented orally by elders. Learning through observation and storytelling, Micmacs grew to adulthood.

In the nineteenth century, non-Indian traditions and procedures were introduced to the Micmac. Between 1820 and 1843 the Governor and Council of Nova Scotia passed several acts creating Indian reserves regulated by the province. When Nova Scotia joined the Confederation of Canada in 1867, regulation of Micmac affairs was transferred to the federal government.

Prior to World War II, a small number of Micmac families had migrated to the New England States, particularly to Massachusetts, where they settled in Lowell, Revere, Haverhill, and Boston. A greater number of Micmac Indians moved to Boston in the mid-1960s and early 1970s. Four to five thousand Indians were living in Boston and its suburbs. Construction and manufacturing jobs attracted many, yet by 1979 unemployment was high. In 1979 , fifty-five percent of Boston's Indian males and forty-five percent of its Indian women over sixteen did not have full-year employment. Median household income was $7,191 compared to $12,530 for the population as a whole.

Canadian Micmacs needing help frequently encountered problems obtaining jobs or receiving government benefits and services because *their rights under the 1794 Jay Treaty between Great Britain and the United States were misunderstood. International treaties and current U.S. law permit Canadian-born Indians to cross the Canada-U.S. border freely, live and work in the United States (although they may not be employed by the federal, state, or local government), and obtain such public benefits as unemployment compensation and food stamps. Canadian-born Natives living in the United States do not have to have an alien card ("green card"), register as an alien, or obtain a work permit. Although the Jay Treaty was ratified over two hundred years ago, the rights derived from it are still misunderstood or ignored by many public and private agencies.*

Most Micmacs who came to Boston were Catholic. The Micmacs had been christianized by missionaries in the seventeenth century. (Membertou, a Micmac chief, and one hundred and forty followers were baptized at Port Royal in 1610.) For centuries Micmac social life had centered around church activities, including the celebration of Church Feast Days (which only seem to direct attention to the pathos of life on the reserve).

In 1972 a Native American Indian center opened in Boston in 1972 to serve the native population. Dependent solely on federal funding for its operation, it rarely received funds for emergency use. Nevertheless, the center's social worker arranged with other city service organizations to fill the needs that the center could not.

As similar Native American centers sprang up in major cities throughout the United States and Canada in the early seventies, a network known as the "Moccasin telegraph" became an important system of communicating information to the Native population.

Native American men and women who were afflicted with the disease of alcoholism lived and slept in the city streets. They did not use a shelter that was available to them because they feared the system. In the winter of 1976, an Indian woman froze to death in an abandoned building in the inner city.

Anne woke up abruptly. She heard her husband Morris and her two brothers, Greg and James, talking and laughing in the next room. Their loud chatter had awakened her. She didn't hear her babies, however; they were still sleeping. The room was cold, damn cold in the Canadian winter. She could see the mist of her breath. She didn't want to get up. She stretched her limbs and felt her muscles tighten. She groaned, let out a big sigh, and shuddered as she remembered how her brother Johnny looked in the courtroom the day before when the judge sentenced him to Waterloo Penitentiary for ten years.

Then she got out of bed, gathered up her clothes, dressed, and went into the kitchen.

Morris was putting the coffee pot on the stove to boil. "I don't know what is going to happen today," he remarked. "Johnny is being sent to that prison. Everyone we know is blaming us, too—for what he did. They are mad. They say it is our fault too."

Greg came in the back door carrying an armful of wood. He hollered, "We better think about getting more wood stacked up. We don't have enough to last the winter."

James crossed the room and opened the door. He stood in the opening and excitedly yelled out to them, "Hey, you guys! There is a bunch of people coming along the road. It looks like they are heading this way."

Anne said, "Shut the goddamn door, it's freezing in here!" A cold blast of air hit the warm kitchen.

Anne thought, *I know there was a hell of a lot of commotion at the trial. What are they up to now?*

She walked to the window, wiped the frosted glass with a circular motion, and looked out. "Jeez, what is that crowd doing gathered out there?"

A group of people, all bunched together, were standing in front of the house. Even in the early daylight, they looked grim and formidable. Anne was frightened by the look of them.

Peering over her shoulder, Morris observed, "The chief and constable are there too." He walked over to the door and opened it.

Anne followed him and hollered out to the crowd, "What do you guys want? Has something happened?"

She stood in front of Morris. Framed together in the doorway, they waited for someone to reply. Her brothers stood there too, waiting to hear what this was all about.

Dan Thunder, a big, robust man and the reserve's policeman, stood in front of the crowd. Anne and Morris had known him all their lives. This morning, Dan looked as if he had dressed in haste. His winter cap was skewed on top of his head, and his heavy gray coat was unbuttoned. Stepping forward, he hesitated for a moment, then cleared his throat. In a strong, forceful voice Dan Thunder ordered Anne and Morris off the reserve.

In the frozen air Dan's command came across clearly to Anne and Morris: "You have to get off the reserve right now ! If you don't get off right now," Dan ordered, "we will burn your house and everything in it and you too, if you are still here."

Anne caught her breath at the viciousness of the threat. She turned and faced Morris. They stared into each other's eyes. It was just for a moment, but it seemed like an eternity. The two of them had grown up on the reserve, as had their ancestors. It was the only way of life they had ever known. Anne had gone to the Indian boarding school for a few years, and both she and Morris had gone to work in the blueberry fields in Maine. Occasionally, they went off the reserve to visit family and friends on other reserves and to do their basic shopping in a small town. The reserve was their life. It was basically a part of them. It was where family and traditional values existed. It was where the tribe celebrated St. Anne's Day in a grand and glorious fashion. It was where spear-fishing for eel at night by flashlight heralded in a new season.

Anne said, "Come on, let's go, then."

They quickly packed a few belongings, picked up their two small kids, walked to the car, and piled in. The Chief and Dan Thunder escorted them to the edge of the reserve, where they were stopped. Chief Elliot Lee, who had been elected "chief" for five consecutive years and who was judged by the community as a fair and honest man, came over to their car and motioned Morris to open the car window.

He leaned down. "You are banished from this reserve for five years. Do not come back here until then."

Morris shut the car window, started the engine, and headed for the main highway. Anne was stunned by the events that had transpired. Everything had happened so fast. She felt as if she were moving in slow motion, as if in a nightmare.

She glanced around the car at her husband next to her and her two brothers in back. She saw the grim expressions on their faces, reflecting what she was feeling. They all knew the tribal law. They knew that rape, murder, and larceny were the reasons given for banishment from the reserve. The "Chief" and his council must have met last night and, finding them responsible for the act that Anne's brother had committed, agreed to this punishment.

Morris remained quiet, as if he were thinking. Then he spoke up. "Well, what do you say? What shall we do? Where shall we head for? How much money have we got?"

Greg and James dug into their pockets. Anne replied, " I have forty-five dollars I was saving to buy some spring clothes."

Morris answered, "That should take us to Boston. I have a few dollars, twenty to be exact."

The brothers spoke up as one, "We have a few dollars, maybe twenty between us."

"Good!" Morris exclaimed. "You can buy the hamburgers when we stop to rest." They drove all afternoon and into the night.

The winter sun was breaking over the horizon as they entered Boston. The sky was gray, with a touch of pink lining the edges. They drove around the strange city streets. Looking for a phone, they saw a convenience store open. Anne went in and flipped through the pages of the telephone book. She was impatient and began fumbling, turning the pages hurriedly as she skimmed the book looking for a familiar name. She had to find someone she could call for help. She was hoping to find her Uncle Wilson Johns' number.

Wilson had left the reserve four years before, but last year had brought his family back to the reserve for a visit. He had given them information about Boston and news about people they knew who had left the reserve. He said they were making out okay. Their cousin Paul was in jail; May and her kids were on welfare.

Hey, thought Anne, *maybe May has a phone but her number is not listed.* She shrugged and remembered what had happened last year when Wilson's brother had gone to Maine to pick blueberries and had been killed by a hit-and-run driver. When the officials from the States called the reserve looking for Wilson, the family told them that he was in Boston. They knew he had been contacted. He must have a phone, Anne said to herself, but she could not find Wilson listed—or anyone else she knew. She was worried. Giving up her search, she returned to the car.

There they sat quietly, smoking. Someone cracked open a window and cold air rushed in.

Anne mentioned, "We heard there was an Indian center in Boston. If we could find it, maybe they would help us."

Morris went back into the store and asked the clerk if he knew about an Indian community. The clerk did not know but he had responded excitedly, "Si, si," when asked if he knew about an Indian center in Boston.

He said, "I pass it all the time," he said. I live in Jamaica Plain. When I am on the bus, I see a building that has a sign on it. It says 'American Indian Spoken Here'."

The clerk gave Morris directions to the center. "When you get to Huntington Avenue, you will pass an Indian on a horse. Keep on going and you will come to it."

They drove by the center and waited for it to open. When the first employee entered the building, they rushed out of the car and entered the building. The receptionist asked the family where they were from.

Anne answered, "We are from the Clear Lake Reserve in Canada. We need to speak to someone."

The receptionist airily told them, "You have to wait for the social worker to come in." She motioned to the waiting room. "You can wait in there. She will be in soon. Someone will be making coffee shortly."

The blue plastic chairs in the waiting room were uncomfortable, but everyone was tired, and the warmth of the room was hypnotic. Anne nodded and, giving in to her tiredness, dozed.

In her reverie, Anne was a kid again, sitting on a stoop with her grandfather in the cool evening light in front of their shack. Her grandfather's voice was low and soothing as he told Anne stories about when he was a young man and how he went away from the reserve to join the Canadian army in the First World War.

Anne asked him, "Why?"

"So did a lot of other Micmacs join up," he answered. "When we came back, if we were caught with fish or deer meat, we were sent to jail in Halifax."

Anne again asked why.

"I don't know why they did that to us. I never thought we could do anything about it. We were trapped on this reserve, just like the animals we caught"

Anne then asked her father, "Who trapped us?" But before her father could answer, Anne felt herself being shaken. It was Morris.

"What are we going to do? The kids are getting hungry. I haven't seen anyone I know."

Anne asked the people who came into the center that morning if they had seen Jeff, her oldest son who had come to Boston two years earlier.

Anne remained silent. She looked into the gym where the kids were playing. Anne's brothers were sprawled against the wall.

"Gosh damn, I don't know," Anne answered. "I guess we should wait to talk to the social worker."

A woman came rushing into the building. She commented to the receptionist, " I'm sorry I am late, but I got caught in traffic on the Fellsway. I don't know why they schedule these early morning meetings the way out of hell and back."

The receptionist motioned to the family. "There are some people here to see you. They're from the Clear Lake Reserve in Canada."

The woman greeted them. "Hello, my name is Jane. I'm a Navajo and social worker for the center. Come with me."

The family followed her down a long hallway that had tiny offices on one side. She led them into one of the offices, saying, "Sorry, I don't think I can fit you all in here." The kids and the two teenagers were sent back to the gym to wait.

Anne looked into the room; It was painted a light yellow. Indian-design curtains hung on the tiny window. Posters on the wall blazoned, "Save Peltier" and "Remember Wounded Knee." An oil painting on the wall behind Jane's desk depicted an Indian paddling a birchbark canoe through white water. The artist had captured the stirring movements of the wild, capricious rapids.

In a low and trembling voice Anne told the social worker about the events that had brought her family to the city. It wasn't an easy story to tell. Jane had to lean forward to hear what Anne was saying.

"My brother accidentally killed a young girl on the reserve. It happened at my house. We were having a party. My brother and the girl had an argument, and he pushed her. She fell and hit her head on the stove. It was an accident. We had to leave the reserve. We have no money and no place to stay."

Anne described her family who were with her: "Two brothers and two children. My babies are three and four years old. I do have an older son who is twenty," she added. "I have heard from him from time to time, but I haven't seen him since he left the reserve three years ago. The last news I got about him was that he was in Boston. His name is Jeff, I have been asking the people I met this morning about him."

Jane called the director of the center who came down to meet the family. Jay Roberts was a tall, lean, and lanky man with blond hair. He was a Sioux. Four generations back, his great-grandfather had been a registered member of the Oglala Sioux. Jay was also a trained lawyer. He greeted Anne's family, then listened attentively as Jane related their problems. The director casually suggested to Jane that she could make arrangements for the family to stay at a hotel for several nights. Jane made the call, then gave the family directions on how to get there. It was in the skid row section of Boston, and part of the directions to it went winding around in Anne's head.

Jane continued, "The hotel is about four blocks past Indian Park."

"How will I know when I get to Indian park?" Anne asked.

Jane tossed off the remark. "You will see Indians drinking on the benches. Some might be passed out on the pavement".

Anne tried to understand why the social worker would say something like that.

It was early afternoon when the family left the center. They were tired and hungry. All they had in their stomachs was the coffee they had drunk at the center. Anne had fixed a cup with cream and sugar and poured a tiny bit of coffee in it for the children.

They found the hotel located in the skid row section of the city. It was a run-down, four-story brick building. They parked the car and walked into the hotel. The desk clerk, who was expecting them, said, "We have two rooms for you."

They walked up the stairs and into a room that smelled of musty, stale air. Gray- white shades, relics of the past, hung dimly on the window, shutting out the gray winter light. Nevertheless, the room appeared warm. An old fashioned radiator hissed and clanked out a cheerful sound.

James and Greg began to talk about their journey. Anne just as quickly told her brothers, "You guys have to go out and buy some food. Buy some baloney and bread, and get some milk for the kids, and a bottle of pop for us."

The family was safe. They were together. With those thoughts in her head, Anne climbed wearily onto the bed and stretched out fully dressed. She lay there half-awake, half-dreaming or dozing. Perhaps she was just plain scared to death.

Images of her past floated beneath Anne's consciousness and surfaced into her thoughts. She was at school, standing in line while waiting for the Sister to spoon out a teaspoonful of cod liver oil. She was a kid. She swallowed the fishy, oily tasting stuff with one gulp. She sat in her seat in the classroom, looking out the window to see the budding leaves on the tree. She was struck by their beauty, by their lime-green color, by the way they were tightly curled together.

Anne leaned over and whispered to a classmate. The class hadn't started. She quickly moved and got up when the Sister's harsh voice ordered her to go to the cloakroom. Anne spent the morning in there waiting. She attempted to defend herself. She spoke to her in small voice, "I didn't do anything. I didn't do anything."

She held out her hand and waited for the ruler to come down. She did not know why she was being punished. The Sister did not say anything. She did not explain. Still puzzled, Anne left school and walked home When she opened the door of her home, she saw her mother standing by the kitchen table kneading flour dough.

Suddenly Anne came to with the screeching sounds of a siren as a fire engine roared past.

They had been in the city for two weeks. It was now the middle of January. Piles of dirty snow, left over from a late winter storm the week before, were everywhere—a striking contrast to the white, pristine look of snow back on the reserve.

Anne looked around the city in shock. She stood with her family on the street corner. She held the few bundles of clothing they owned. They had been locked out of their room.

"Let's head back to the center."

They drove away in silence. Even the children remained quiet. When they came to Harrison Avenue and drove over the potholes, they were jolted out of their reverie. From the back seat, Greg and James said in unison, "What the hell is this?" Together, they all laughed uproariously.

Anne groaned and remarked, "I hope the car doesn't break down."

When they arrived at the center the receptionist informed them that Jane was at a meeting. "She will see you this afternoon when she gets back."

The family walked past the receptionist and into the gym, pulled down some chairs from the stacked deck, and carried them over to a table. They had gone without food that morning. What money they had come to Boston with had long since gone.

They sat clustered around the table, talking in dull tones as a note of resignation crept in their voices. No one offered them coffee. James walked out of the gym and came back with a lighted cigarette in his hand. It was passed around. Each person took a drag, inhaled, and blew out the smoke in defiant gestures. Some of the staff people who walked through the hall lifted their hands in a slight gesture, reluctantly acknowledging the family's presence. They knew they themselves could not help, as they were working for low pay and had their own immediate family and relatives living with them. The small apartments they lived in were already overcrowded.

Suddenly, the smell of food seemed to filter throughout the building. The family went down to the basement where the kitchen was located. There, six Indian elders of the city came together to have lunch: six box lunches—meager portions, as the elders well knew—supplied by a city agency.

Paper cups with six tea bags were spread out on the table. An Ojibway woman, an elder, called out to the family, "You can share my tea bag with me. I drink weak tea." Anne accepted the offer. She made a cup of tea with sugar and milk and gave it to the children to drink.

The kitchen was the center of activity. The young Indian men and women who staffed the infants and toddlers' unit and the Head Start program hustled around the room preparing food. A child and a baby were carried into the room and handed over to the elders so that the younger people could work.

A woman came up to Anne and quietly spoke to her as she pushed on past. "If there is any food left over, we can give it to you."

The family sat in the midst of the crowded space, patiently waiting for the room to clear out, and for the promised food to appear. Later in the afternoon, a young women brought out a plate of spaghetti and a few slices of bread.

Several people came into the room on their afternoon break. The family got more cigarettes from them. Anne asked again about Jeff.

One person said, "Oh, I heard he went down to Virginia last month with a German broad. I think they are working on a marijuana farm down there. They wanted me to go with them but I didn't go. I didn't want to mess around with that stuff."

Anne wondered what he was talking about. She knew some of the young people had brought marijuana back to the reserve, but how and where it grew and whether it was legal or not she did not know. She thought, *Now I am worried about Jeff. I hope he isn't in trouble.*

It was late in the afternoon when Jane met again with Anne and Morris. Anne reminded her that they didn't have a place to sleep that night and also had no money. She continued to tell her the problems they were having in contacting their uncle. She heard that he had moved out of the city to Haverhill, just as their friend May had. They could not get in touch with either of them.

While continuing to reassure them, Jane explained that the center had exhausted their emergency funds. "We can get you in to the city shelters," she told Anne. "You and the children can go to a women's shelter, and the guys can go to a men's shelter."

Anne and Morris faced each other. Speaking in their language, their conversation turned into a mild disagreement.

They finally turned back to Jane. Anne looked directly at the social worker and said, "We can't be split up."

The family slept in the car that night.

Weeks later, there wasn't even the car. They were all sleeping on the ground under the expressway.

Anne eventually moved into an apartment in Dorchester and was there for five years before she returned to her reserve in Canada. Morris died on the streets of Boston three years after he arrived in the city.

Joanne Dunn

3 ~🌾

Joanne's Story

Joanne Dunn is a Micmac woman who is presently acting director of the Native American Indian Community Center of Boston (formerly the Boston Indian Council). Her goal, now that she has reached mid-life, is to continue with her education, enjoy her grandchildren, and continue to support the Native American Center of Boston. Unfortunately, in 1997, when the interview with her was made, the center's work was diminished as a result of a lack of federal funding. Just a few programs were in operation.

On the late winter day I left my Back Bay apartment to interview her, the sky was glazed with gray clouds and the winds blowing down from Canada were cold and strong. I struggled to keep my balance on the windswept street before I entered the stairs that led down to the underground subway system. When I entered the center the receptionist called Joanne to tell her I was there. Climbing the stairs to her third-floor office was difficult: I was ten years older than when I started this book! Joanne's interview follows:

I was born in Maine in 1948 and moved with my family to Boston when I was eight. My mother is registered to Wagmatcook, a Micmac reserve located on Cape Breton Island, Canada. I am registered to that same reserve as well as with the reservation of the Aroostook Band of Micmacs in Maine. The band has just been federally recognized.

Mother's spiritual essence, the inner strength and peace she projected in her life, has always influenced me and compelled me to be judgmental about my own. My parents were married for twenty-eight years. I am the oldest of their nine children.

My mother's mother died when she was seventeen, leaving Mother without a family since her brothers and sisters were sent to an Indian boarding school. Mother also left the reserve at that time, accompanied by two girl friends. Filled with adventure, they went off to work in the blueberry fields in Maine. In late fall, when the migrant season was over, the three girls decided to remain in the United States. They arrived in Boston in 1945. A year later, when she was eighteen, my mother married my father, who worked in the trades as a skilled machinist. He was a good provider, but as his work was transient we were constantly on the move to the various job sites he held in the Boston area and elsewhere in New England. Father always brought his family with him and, as a result, his children were always in the process of changing schools.

I felt I was out of place and just knew I never belonged in any of the schools I had to attend. One memory I recall is of Mother making sandwiches for my school lunches. She made them out of *luskinakin* (Indian biscuits), and they were thick! I remember trying to mash them down to appear like Wonder Bread. As much as I changed schools back then, it did not bother me; I always felt the strong support and devotion that Mother had for me and her family. When I entered kindergarten at age six, I already knew how to read. Mother had taught me, as she believed in education. However, in spite of this tremendous start, I became a high-school dropout when I was a teenager. I married early and had three children. I now have five grandchildren. Before I married I attended a training course on microfiche technology. After completing the course I eventually went to work for a bank.

Up until 1972 my association with Indian people was limited to neighbors of Micmac descent and to Mother's brothers and sisters, who came on annual visits from the reserves in Canada. In 1972 I went to work at the Boston Indian Council, where I met fellow members of Indian tribes who came from both Canada and the United States.

I soon became aware that I was bereft of Indianness. I had little knowledge of my tribe or my Indian heritage. I have learned about my tribe's history since then, however, and throughout the years I have participated in traditional Indian rituals while remaining a member of the Catholic church.

In 1972 I was assigned to work in the finance department of the Boston Indian Council. Because I lacked bookkeeping experience I enrolled in a course at Northeastern University. This began a pattern of taking a course on occasion at Northeastern University that continued for many years. In 1991 Radcliffe Seminars, a program within Radcliffe College, was recruiting minorities for a business administration course. I applied, was accepted into the program, and in 1994 obtained a certificate in advanced administration.

My commitment to the Boston Indian Council and the Indian community has never wavered since my association began in 1972. I have remained steadfast to the cause. Throughout the years I have celebrated many joyous festivities at the center, and, sadly enough, in 1987 weathered the rough times of a bankruptcy the organization underwent.

One of the most unusual and profound experiences in my life happened six years after I became affiliated with the Boston Indian Council. It happened during the "Longest Walk" that took place in Washington, D.C. in 1978. I was with the contingent from Boston and among the twenty thousand Indian people who walked from the Green Belt Park in Maryland to Washington, D.C. When we arrived in a specific area in Washington I joined a crowd of people. There an Indian touched my hand and guided me into a group "for Indians only." I was touched by the feeling it generated. It made me feel proud. Feeling and being "Indian" had never hit close to home before, but in an instant I felt and sensed a feeling of belonging I had never felt before. The "Longest Walk" will remain in my heart forever.

One shattering experience the community shared happened as a result of an interview the center's staff willingly granted a reporter whose paper was based in Cambridge. When the reporter came to the center we felt it was an opportunity to get positive media exposure. The directors graciously gave the reporter a tour of the center while explaining to him the functions of the various in-house programs. He seemed impressed by the work the center was doing and took more than a casual interest in the "Tiny Tots and Babies" program, which was basically designed for both working mothers and mothers who were studying for their general high school equivalency diploma. At least, so we thought the reporter was interested in the program. He had a cheerful personality and was smiling as he sat and scribbled his notes.

When he completed his mission, the staff anxiously awaited the edition of the paper in which the story was to appear. But when the community saw the story he wrote, we were shocked. We were angry to see in print a negative report on the center: a story of alcoholism and how the disease affected an Indian family. This was a judgmental view. We all felt betrayed. Obviously the reporter had choices. At that time, in 1972, when the center's efforts to create change for the Indians of Boston began, leaders of the community realized that the city's service agencies were not in touch with Indians and therefore no special effort was being made to address the needs of the Indian population. The programs initiated at the center in 1972 were the first in New England to serve native people. The opening of the Boston Indian Council was an historic event. Apparently the reporter's and the publisher's social consciousness did not allow them to record a view of "the renascence" of Indian country nationwide.

Despite that episode, reflections of my Indian Council experience during the years 1972-1991 are highlighted with positive stories. Thousands of Native American Indians have passed through the doors of the center throughout the twenty-five years it has been in operation. The center's federally-funded programs have included those for housing, health, and education as well as a half-way house for alcoholics. Community people of all ages took advantage of the education program. They obtained their high school diplomas; some went on to college and other training programs. (After getting her GED, my own mother went on to take several college courses in early childhood education to qualify for a certificate allowing her to work in a children's program. She worked with the children of the community until she retired in 1989.) Others gained work experience and went on to better themselves in the job market, while some trained in an electronics program and eventually worked in that field. Some people, trained in office procedures or experienced in community politics, returned to their reserves as skilled office workers and advocates for social change. One person became Chief of his reserve when he returned and remains in that titled position today. The Indian Council Community Center was also a setting where young people met. Romance blossomed and many intertribal marriages were performed!

Joanne's Favorite Glooskap Story

A long time ago there were three young Indians who had three different wishes. One day as they were sitting around their campfire, they decided to go and see Glooskap and ask him to grant their wishes. So the three *Ulnoog* (Indian men) began their search for Glooskap. The way was not easy, for they first had to cross through the Great Serpents, a mythical valley of fear

The three Ulnoog were hungry and had to eat, so one went for food and was rewarded by a catch of deer. They went on until they came to the great slamming mountains that stood in front of their path. This was the way to the great Glooskap. But they had to be careful, because no one knew when the mountains would slam together!

At last their journey came to an end. There in front of them were three wigwams. They had come into the village of the three wigwams. There they saw the first of the three people. His name was Earthquake. They looked into the next wigwam and saw one Indian lying on the ground. He couldn't move because he had no bones, but, by order of Glooskap, he would be shifted around; each move caused the seasons to change. The third wigwam they saw was filled with light, a bright light that overcame them. It was the Spirit of Love.

The three Ulnoog came back to Earthquake to ask if Glooskap would see them. Earthquake talked to Glooskap. "There are three people to see you."

Glooskap replied, "I know what they want. They have three wishes."

Earthquake told Glooskap that one wanted to be big and tall; the second wanted to be free from all sickness; and the third wanted to be free from problems.

Glooskap told Earthquake to bring them to the cliffs and stand them there. There they are still. On a windy day you can hear them speak.

One says, "Oh, how tall and strong I am!" The second one says, "Oh, how great I feel!" And the third one says, "Oh, how free I am!"

Glooskap, you see, had transformed the men into trees.

4 ⟞⟨⟨⟨⟨

Rita's Story

*I*n 1987, while I was an Urban Community Fellow at M.I.T., I seriously thought about writing after I interviewed Rita. I began my
school project by asking her if I could document her story. She was
agreeable to the idea and gave her consent. After the interviews, I asked
her why she had been so frank and outspoken. She replied rather vehe-
mently, "I want other Indian women to know what happened!"

As part of British Indian policy, a tract of land was awarded in the
utter wilderness of Nova Scotia to a Micmac tribe. This reserve (as
reservations are called in Canada) was named the Millbrook Reserve
and lay alongside the Shubinakie River, where the tribe had access to
its abundant water resources and fertile soil.

European immigrants to Canada in the late eighteenth-century
flocked to the wilderness of Nova Scotia and settled a town across the
river from the Millbrook Reserve. As the population of the town
increased, more land was needed for expansion. In 1900 Canadian law
forced the tribal people and the reservation from its location to a new
site five miles inland.

The move created hardships for the people that lasted for decades,
as the people of the reserve were now essentially without a primary
source of food. They could no longer fish in the Shubinakie River in the
traditional way of their forefathers, and they no longer had access to the
rich fertile soil along the riverbank. Pictures taken on the reserve at that
time depict the people as looking thin, gaunt, and emaciated.

If you think, "What could possibly get worse for them?"—then
,think again. This is what happened: The situation worsened because
the fishing and hunting laws came into being in Canada and included
the tribal people as well, despite the treaties that protected the North
American Indians' hunting and fishing rights. Now, when the people of

the reserve were caught fishing and hunting out of season, they were charged and convicted of a federal offense and sent to prison. The people of the reserve were at the mercy of the Canadian government, under the rule of the British Empire. The people no longer had a source of food, other than what meager rations (flour) the government doled out to them. Food vouchers were given to them enabling them to get just the barest of necessities.

It was cold. The blizzard winds blasted down from the north and invaded the tar paper shack. The black iron potbelly stove shed its warmth in a circle of light. A baby cried; its fiery sound stretched out to encompass the sounds of the wind.

I was born in 1932 on the Millbrook Reserve in Canada. The reserve contained ten acres of land and was without a water system or electricity. The year I was born there were a hundred people registered on the tribal rolls.

The Indian agent assigned to the reserve by the Canadian government lived in a wood-frame house on the outskirts of the reserve. There he supervised the social structure of the reserve and its tribal people and generally maintained law and order.

His other duties included the distribution of food vouchers. He was also responsible for obtaining used clothing, which he distributed to the people as well. He was authorized to obtain medical services for the community when needed. Medical care on the reserve was limited, and only in extreme emergencies was a doctor brought in from town to treat serious illness. Accident cases were taken by car and train to a hospital thirty miles from the reserve.

The introduction of Christianity to the Native People of America is recorded as happening as early as 1610. Seemingly, my ancestors were converted to Christianity when the first wave of missionaries arrived in the New World.

A Catholic church was built on the reserve when it was first moved inland. The priest assigned to it lived in a wood-frame house on the edge of the reserve. He also supervised the social structure of the reserve, and took care of the spiritual needs of the people. He arranged the placement of Micmac children in Indian boarding schools when it became necessary.

The social activities of the reserve centered around the church. The people celebrated "Indian Day" by holding pie socials. The women used berries that grew wild and flour from their scant supplies to bake pies, auctioning them to the members of the community for a nickel or a dime. The money made by the auction was then eagerly donated to the church building fund. The people of the reserve also celebrated a Catholic ritual: St. Anne's Feast Day. They paraded through the reserve carrying a statue of Saint Anne. Now it is generally known that the Micmac women who were first converted to Catholicism incorporated Indian clothing into Catholic rituals. They designed and created original beaded caps, copying the headdress worn by the nuns in the eighteenth century. Another festive occasion for the community to celebrate was the birth of a baby. Baptism was a ritual observed. It was the custom that if you had money, you pressed a dollar bill into the baby's hands. The women of the reserve also met and held weekly sewing circles.

At that time the reserve was without a source of employment. The men went off the reserve to look for work but rarely found jobs. Since it was in the era of the Great Depression that my story takes place, work was hard to find for everyone. Some Micmac men without an education or skilled training did find work in construction and on road gangs. They also did odd jobs and maintenance work in the town. A few women worked in the town as well.

Early Memories

My first recollections of the reservation begin when I was about four. I remember being in a small shack with my family. The shack was so small that it held just the basic of furnishings: a stove, two wood boxes, a table, and a big bed. Food and other supplies in the shack were stored under the bed. My two brothers and a sister stayed on the bed, since there wasn't enough room in the shack for us on the floor.

I was playing with my six-month-old baby sister. She was gurgling and smiling up at me. Suddenly, a drop of water fell from the ceiling onto her mouth. It was the color purple. I watched as it curled around her lips. She sucked it in and died instantly. I found out later that rainwater collected on the roof of the shack had eroded the tar paper, and drops of water containing toxic substances had leaked down.

Mother

Mother was a tiny, petite women with a light complexion and strong black hair. She had borne ten children. She was an unusual person, I thought, with a complex personality. She was warm and forceful on the reserve, but became timid and fearful when we went off the reserve to a small town nearby. I heard her say many times in my younger years that she did not trust the townspeople. Despite the fears that hounded her, she did make the necessary trips to town, and to the city of St. John when the mayflowers were in season. She spoke English only when it became necessary.

I was six years old the day Mother and I walked on the dusty sidewalks of a small town. I remember being frightened and holding tightly to her hand. The people and the children of the town stopped and turned around to stare at us. It was the way they looked at us that made me feel as if I were nothing but an object. It made me feel like I was an Indian, whatever that is supposed to mean. After we finished shopping it was our custom to drop in at a coffee shop for a snack before returning to the reserve. Mother cautioned me in a stern voice, "Don't touch anything. Don't ask for anything in there!" Then her voice changed, and she leaned down and patted me and said in a soothing tone, "It will be all right."

Mother always spoke up for her rights on the reservation, and sometimes she and the Indian agent gossiped about the happenings on the reserve. Once, I heard them discussing the Indian agent assigned to a nearby reserve. Our agent said to Mother, "I hear the people at Brook River finally got mad at their agent and got rid of him. I would have ordered *him* to stand at attention myself!" Mother responded, "If you ever acted the way he did, I'm sure the people here would not have stood it for long."

It was known throughout the Micmac reserves that the agent assigned to Brook River controlled his people by using military tactics. It seems that the agent enlisted in the army in the Second World War and was trained as a sergeant. Eventually he returned to his post where he continued to act like a soldier. He ordered the people of the reserve to salute him, and he lined them up to stand in formation whenever he distributed the food vouchers.

The Canadian winters were long and cold, with blizzards that blew unceasingly for days on end. So in the early spring when the mayflowers blossomed on the far side of the reserve, we made those days "flower-picking times." Those were happy and festive family occasions. We packed several pans of cold *luskinakin* (biscuits) and a big jug of sweet black tea; but no matter how much we brought, there was never enough to go around. My brother Alex ate twice his fair share. All of us yelled at him to stop being so damn piggish. It never stopped him, and he went right on doing what he did best.

The early spring days were bright and warm. I looked up and contemplated the clouds breaking up and wandering aimlessly off into the horizon. It felt good. It was so good being out in the fresh air that I did a little jig. I somersaulted or whatever on the raw, brown earth. I felt snug and safe as the winds of spring flowed in and around me.

At the end of the day, tired and contented, we straggled home carrying baskets filled with flowers. Aunt Sarah went looking for every tin can and bottle she could find and stuffed flowers in them and stuck them throughout the shack. A heavy, sweet fragrance filled the rooms. We had a large room on ground level; a loft above was used as our sleeping quarters. After supper we helped Mother prepare the flowers for market.

During the height of the Depression in 1932, the Micmac women of Nova Scotia collectively developed a system of marketing their products, including mayflowers. The mayflowers blossomed in the second part of May for two weeks. At that time the women selected buds that were about to bloom, then packed them in wet moss and used dry pine cones to keep the bunches separated. The women carried the flowers to market in a type of basket that had been woven by Micmacs since the recording of Micmac history. The women also made use of the ash wood particular to the region and the reserve to design and create "wood flowers." They wove utility baskets. They created works of art, baskets that are exhibited in Canadian museums today.

A picture of Mother hangs in the railway station in St. John, New Brunswick. It depicts her standing on a street corner holding a basket of flowers.

The women traveled to the streets of two major cities in Nova Scotia, riding the Canadian National Railway free of charge because of the existing agreements between tribal members and railroad officials. Another means used in selling flowers was to send them by Railway Express to Native women living in the cities. Those women, in turn, sold them on a percentage basis. A bunch of flowers sold for five or ten cents, and the baskets sold for twenty-five to fifty cents each.

The money made from the sale of flowers was the only money some women saw in a given year. The money bought food. It bought yard goods to make Easter dresses and occasionally curtains.

This project, created by the imaginative Micmac women, came

from a dire need for survival. It added a reality and a richness and flavor to the dimension of reserve life. This venture portrays the Micmac women's strength and power as they struggled to combat the problems caused by the policies of the British Crown. These official policies, in effect, obliterated the rights and dignity of the North American Indian.

I was nine when Mother took me with her to the city for the first time. One morning we left early and carrying two baskets of flowers, walked five miles to the train station. There we boarded a train. I sat on the green plush seats of the trains and looked out the window to see the green rolling meadows of Nova Scotia flash on past. Ten miles down the line we left the train and climbed the gangplank of a ferry that crossed the bay to Halifax. I stood at the railing and looked out to the wide expanse of water. I tasted the salt in the wind. It was a magnificent sight. I'd never been away from the reserve before, and the strange sights and smells that I took in that day were so powerful that I thought I would surely die of all the excitement.

I ran down the gangplank of the ferry when it docked and walked with Mother on the city streets to our destination. I caught a glimpse of a kid's hat as I passed a store window. It was white and made in the style of a Dutch hat. I wanted it so much that I stopped and threw a tantrum. Mother kept on walking. We finally arrived at a busy intersection of the city where Mother arranged the flowers for sale on the sidewalk. I heard music in the air, over the city traffic. I looked across the street to where a street musician was playing. I don't know why I was so curious but I just had to hear him up close. I wanted to see what instrument he was playing. So, without thinking, I dashed into the street. I was oblivious of the traffic and ran fleetingly across the cobblestone street of the historic city.

A customer bought a bouquet of flowers from me that day and gave me a generous two-dollar tip. I gleefully thought, "I could buy that hat for sure now." Mother, however, convinced me the extra money was needed to buy lunch and to bring extra groceries back home with us. I had a big red apple for lunch that day, and as I bit into it, juice dribbled down my chin. With a quick gesture I used my sleeve to wipe it away and looked up and grinned at Mother. I said in Indian, "It is good." And it was! We rarely, if ever, had fresh fruit on the reserve. However, we had a good share of blueberries and blackberries when they were in season.

I was twelve years old when the shack next to our home burned to the ground. Mother watched in horror as her daughter and young sister perished in the flames. She collapsed. She never completely recovered, for she remained a fragile person throughout the rest of her life.

My family life broke up as a result of the tragedy and I was sent with my brothers and sisters to an Indian boarding school run by the Canadian government. We did not see each other often, as we did not return home at the same time. Some of my siblings visited other family members.

I was twelve years old when I arrived at the school. My first impression of the nuns in their black and white habits was that they were pure, holy, and godlike. The children at the school related to me that when if you ran away and were caught and brought back the punishment was that the sisters would cut off all your hair.

Mother came to visit me once in the four years I spent at the school. She came in September on a day that was bright and clear. The transformed leaves were masses of burning color. We went walking on an unused road in back of the school, squashing the dry leaves underfoot and kicking them on ahead. A strong, gusty wind rushed through, scattering the leaves all over the place. We brushed them off and headed back to the school, to the visiting room, to a small space that smelled of carbolic acid disinfectant. We sat on the wood benches and spoke in our language. (The children in school were forbidden to speak in Micmac, their native tongue.) There Mother gave me news of relatives and home. We laughed a lot. At noon, we walked down the long bleak corridor to the lunchroom. My mother had her arm in a sling; she had broken it the week before. I had to help her cut the small piece of meat she was served. I saw she was hungry, for she ate quickly and finished everything on her plate.

When she left I ran to the window to get another glimpse of her as she walked slowly down the road. I wanted to run after her, to go with her and take care of her. But I stood at the window, rooted to the spot. I was too afraid to try. The thought of being bald stopped me from attempting to run off with Mother that day. I remembered, too, what happened to the brother and sister who ran away the first winter I spent at the school. Their bodies were found when the snows melted in the spring, huddled together in a ridge near the school. My twelve-year-old mind rationalized that the nuns would surely go to hell for their meanness.

Grandmother

Grandmother lived in a small shack across the field from us.
Sometimes when it got dark and I looked across the field, I would
see the light from her lamp burning in the window. The light glowing in the dusk often beckoned me to visit her. As I ran toward it, it
was like a beacon that showed me the way. I spent a lot of time with
her until she died when I was eight. She always encouraged me to
attend school no matter what. In the winter, when the snow drifts
were piled high, she had my brothers carry me on their backs to
school. In the evenings in her shack we worked by lamplight, weaving the hooked rugs she was noted for. My job was to hold the roll
of wool she was working with.

She attempted to keep a few chickens once. On mornings when
the temperature dropped, Grandmother bundled me up, tugged a
wool hat over my head, wound a scarf around me, and sent me out
to the chicken coop. I remember how it felt: the sheer bliss of coming back into the warm shack after being out in the freezing cold. I
was real proud carrying the few eggs I had gathered. Grandmother
had to kill the chickens for food.

On the days that Grandmother went to the city to sell the flowers, she got up before sunrise, lit a fire in the stove to make herself
a cup of tea, packed some cold *luskinakin* and left. Some mornings
I stood at the door and waved and hollered out goodbye to her. I
watched her walk down the old dirt road. She turned and wave
back. She usually wore long skirts, topped with big oversized
sweaters, and a hat that was faded and battered out of shape. I'd first
seen it on her when she got it; then it was bright and fresh like the
yellow dandelions that sprinkled the grass in the early spring. It was
the day my family moved into our new home.

The one-room shack my family lived in had became too small
for a family of six. The Canadian government supplied my father
with materials to build a larger shack. They gave him aluminum foil,
tar paper, wood slats, and nails. The aluminum foil prevented the tar
paper from ripping when nailed to the wood slats.

The day the shack was finished I happened to be standing with
my grandmother a distance away on the rise of a hill. The cluster of
faded brown shacks in the background contrasted greatly with my
parents' new, two-level tar shack that towered over them. Narrow
strips of silver aluminum foil, sticking out from the black paper,
shone in the sunlight. From where we stood, the shack was glowing

with silver light! I heard Grandmother draw in a quick breath and exclaim, "Well I'll be damned! It sure does look funny."

The days Grandmother went to the city to sell flowers, her grandchildren waited patiently throughout the afternoon for her return. In the late afternoon my brothers and sisters played outside. We hollered to each other as we looked down the road, and we vied with each other to be the first to catch a glimpse of her. "Do you see her? Is she coming?" we asked each other? When we finally did see her in the distance, all of us kids raced to meet her. As she came close into view, we saw that she was limping, and that her baskets were filled with bundles. We jostled with each other to carry the baskets the rest of the way home. Sometimes we hadn't eaten all day, and we knew that Grandmother always brought back food and a treat for us. The treat was always a bag of round white peppermints. Sometimes she brought back other things that someone in the city gave her.

When winter came and the blizzards blasted through the countryside, we often were snowbound for days. After the storm passed, my brothers, sisters, and I struggled through the snow drifts to visit Grandmother. When we got to her shack we were covered with snow and freezing cold. We quickly whipped our shoes off to warm our feet against the heat of the stove. Some of my brothers didn't have socks on, and you could see their feet bright red from the cold. Grandmother jumped up and brought out her old sewing machine, then dug into a knapsack and came up with used sweaters someone in the city gave her. The sewing machine she used was so old—I'm sure it was the first one ever invented! I don't know where the hell she got it, except maybe when she was adopted out. She cut the sleeves off the sweaters and sewed socks right there for the kids. She quickly and adeptly used the rest of the material to make hats and mittens for her grandchildren.

Nothing ever lasted. It was in 1940, when the mayflower season was over, that Grandma became sick. I went out in the fields and picked a pot of blackberries for her. The day was hot and humid. When I returned, the door of her house was open. Mother and two aunts met me at the door, and would not allow me to enter. I regret to this day that I did not see Grandmother before she died. Mother later told me that she had given Grandmother the berries before she passed away that day. I was eight years old and I knew I would miss the love and attention she gave me. I looked across the field to her shack. It was dark and empty. I would miss her.

What I remember most about my grandmother was her wry sense of humor and her ability to get things done. She was a strong, moral woman who spoke out against the abuse of alcohol on the reserve. She had been adopted when she was a baby, and was raised in the non-Indian world. She returned to reservation life when she married. Grandmother had been the medicine woman for our family, using a combination of drugstore elixir and herbal roots to make "Indian medicine." Members of my family were given her brew to drink steaming hot for whatever ailed us.

Family Members

I had nine siblings: five brothers and four sisters. Two brothers died. Our family broke up when I was twelve and never did regroup. I spent time the first eight years of my life with my grandmother. When I was twelve I was sent from the reserve to boarding school and left there at age sixteen to marry.

I had an Uncle James who enlisted in the Navy in the Second World War and never returned to the reservation to live. He stayed away working on road gangs and in general construction. He was away from the reserve for long periods of time. When he returned to visit he always brought presents for us, perhaps a clock or a small radio. It was goods we might otherwise not have had. He bought and drove old cars that were always in need of repair and he was forever working on them. In the summer he drove our family to the state of Maine where we worked in the blueberry and potato fields. He had to make the same trip twice because of our large family.

Father

Father planted vegetables that grew in cold country in our back yard: potatoes, carrots and cabbage. He went hunting in season only, and fished for eel and salmon in the fall as the gaming and fishing laws of Canada were strict. If someone were caught with an illegal cache of fish or game they were sent to jail for six months. As a result, we were often without food. Father went off the reserve looking for employment but rarely ever found work.

Father enlisted in the army in the Second World War and was sent overseas. He spent six months in a German prisoner-of-war camp. His family found him to be a changed person when he returned to Canada four years later. Before he left for the war, he loved life and all growing things, but when he returned he no longer tended a garden. His war experiences haunted him. He remained a silent and morose man and did not socialize on the reserve as he once did. He learned how to make home brew and drank most of it.

My grandfather enlisted in the army in the First World War; my father and uncle in the second World War; and my husband in the Korean War. Being reservation Indians, they did not come under the conscription laws of Canada. The men in my family volunteered to serve in Canada's armed forces.

Husband

In the summer of 1945 I returned home from school for summer vacation and met the man I married. My parents' shack that summer was the gathering place for the teenagers of the reserve to party—listening to a radio and dancing to the music of the forties. We laughed at corny jokes and found everything hilarious. A young man, a stranger, came in with the crowd. I was told his family had transferred to our reserve that winter. He seemed more grown-up than the young men I knew. I found out that he had been away from reservation life for a year. I supposed that was why. When he was fifteen, he had used his brother's birth certificate to enlist in the army. His parents documented his proper age to the appropriate authorities, and he was released from the army a year later.

I was sixteen and in love. The harmony of the earth and all its relations stirred my being. I walked in the night, in the shadows cast by the full moon. The reserve was silent, its voices stilled. It was midnight. The sound of the night creatures filled the air. Crickets and frogs sang in the nearby brook. A night owl whooped somewhere off in the distance. A cool breeze touched my brow. It felt as fine as silken gossamer, like flax taken from the cat-o'-nine-tails I'd played with in the fall of the year.

I remembered when I was eight or thereabouts being in the drugstore with Mother. I pulled away from her to lean against a glass case and looked with wonder at all the colorful boxes there. While I was standing there someone brought out a box and opened it to reveal bars of soap wrapped in rose-colored tissue paper. I smelled the fragrance of flowers.

Now my mind flashed back to that time. I remembered. I'd saved up a few dollars, and I knew I had to buy a box of that soap for this special time. I just knew.

That summer I carried extra buckets of water from the brook to soak luxuriously in the tin tub using bars of perfumed soap.

We were married that year and transferred our alliance to Eagle Springs Reserve, thirty miles from White Rapids. We bought a shack and established ourselves in the community and proceeded to raise a family. We had twelve children in all. Two died. After our second child was born, my husband became less active in the social life of the reserve. He displayed outbursts of temper and went into unexplained rages. He chose friends who abused alcohol, and when he got drunk—which he did often—he was cruel and abusive to me and the children. I was thoroughly disgusted with his actions. I packed up and went back to my reserve with my children.

I was surprised and disappointed at my parents' reaction to my coming home. They did not support me and remained strangely silent. When my husband came to the reserve to bring us back, I returned with him despite the feelings of hopelessness that came over me. It was as if an invisible chain smothered me. These awkward feelings stayed with me throughout the fifteen years we were married.

I became pregnant twelve times, and whenever I told my husband the news, he responded by staring at me with eyes that were cold, blank and expressionless—without emotion.

Despite the way my husband and I got along, I carried a dream. Perhaps we could speak to each other again as we once did. Perhaps we could be friends. I observed other married couples on the reserve and watched how they interacted with each other, how they were raising their children. They seemed to be friends, and seemed to be happy. The dreams and hopes I had for us were never realized.

My husband came from a family of basket weavers. His mother's skill in weaving baskets was such that the baskets she made are exhibited today in the museums in Canada. My husband was trained to look for and select ash trees for their fine grain and for pounding the wood into narrow strips required for basket making. He was a slight and slender man with light brown hair and a rather pale complexion, and could easily pass for white. He had a fifth-grade education and did not have training in any type of skills; therefore, he worked on road construction gangs and did manual labor when he could find work.

When the Korean War broke out in 1952, we had been married for five years and had four children. He enlisted in the Canadian Army and was sent to Korea, returning home three years later a bitter and angry man. He looked for a job but could not find one. In desperation he passed for white and applied for a job with the

Canadian National Railway. He was hired. (The CNR had a policy of not hiring Indians.) For the next two years he lived in constant fear of being found out. One day, a fellow worker overheard him talking in Indian to his friends from the reserve. Rather than face up to his masquerade and the prospect of being fired, he just up and quit the job.

Some summers, my family—that is, my husband and children—went to the potato and blueberry fields in Maine to work. My uncle drove us down in his old car. One summer my husband met a woman at the camp grounds, and did not return home with his family at the end of the season. Well, when I got home I went out and got myself a job in a factory. I was real proud when I received my very first paycheck and cashed it at the local grocery store. I spent all of it on food, and, believe me, the four weeks I worked my family never had it so good. We thoroughly enjoyed all the food the extra money bought.

My husband returned home and that year we migrated to the U.S.A., to Boston, Massachusetts. Again my uncle drove us down in a car that shuddered, smoked, and rattled. A broken window made the long ride cold and hazardous. My oldest daughter remained on the reserve with relatives. My uncle returned immediately to bring the rest of the children down.

Shortly after we arrived, we found a tenement apartment in a working-class neighborhood and my husband went looking for a job. He found part-time work in a meat-packing plant and seasonal work for a roofing company. He never did find a good steady job. I stayed home and cared for my nine children and spent my time bargain shopping for food, and at a local thrift shop.

I watched only entertainment programs on TV, because news of the city and the world somehow did not penetrate my consciousness. I was oblivious of what went on around me. It seemed as if I was holding my breath, existing in a strange place with strange people and customs. It was then that my husband and I compared life on the reservation to life in the city, and we both agreed that to stay in the city was the right thing to do. We summed it up with the idea that at least we had access to food.

I was totally alienated in my new environment—with one exception. I dressed the kids up and faithfully went to church with them every Sunday, and I made a special effort to have a nice lunch for them and a treat on that day. In the summer I made them a batch of Kool-Aid; in the winter hot cocoa to go with their meal.

One Christmas, things looked very bleak for us. My husband was out of work on workmen's compensation. That year I'd hoped to make a Christmas for the children with a present for each of them, but if that was to happen now I would have to go out looking for a job. Three weeks before Christmas, I found work. I was indeed happy as a lark as I sat at a workbench in an electronics plant, because I knew I would get a paycheck before Christmas.

During the three years we spent in the city we went once, just once, on a family outing to the beach. We never had the nickels for bus fare for nine kids. One summer we went twice to a park to watch an Indian team play softball, and again my uncle came in the summer several times and treated the kids to ice cream cones as we sat on the front stoop watching the kids play in the street.

We tried for three years to make a go of it in Boston. We did our best to make it work, as we did not want to return to the reserve. But the problems we encountered in the city increased. Unemployment, hunger, loss of jobs, accidents, evictions, and other afflictions associated with emotional stress and illness were experienced. We finally gave up and returned to the reserve.

Three months later my husband died, leaving me a widow with ten children. Being strong and healthy I decided to go to work and found a job in a rug factory near the reserve. I was employed for about three months. I had opened a bank account and saved up a few dollars, and at the urging of friends who had recently moved to Lynn, Massachusetts, I moved back to the United States.

On My Own

I packed a few clothes and hired a neighbor and his car to drive me and the kids to the States. My oldest daughter chose to remain on the reserve with relatives. The car was filled with the children, myself and the driver. When we stopped at a toll bridge outside of Boston, the collector looked in the car and saw the nine kids jampacked in the back seat and said jokingly, "Why don't you leave a couple of the kids here? "

My friends rented a furnished apartment for me in Lynn and after I settled in, I immediately went looking for work. My friends' oldest daughter would baby-sit the children. I was interviewed for a job, took an aptitude test, and passed it with a high score. I was hired and told to report for work the next week. The next day, however, I received a call from the receptionist who told me that the company could not hire me, as I was not a citizen of the United States. I received the call at a public phone located in the street outside the apartment building. I did not know my rights then as a North American Indian; otherwise I might have spoken up for the job.

Two months later my friends moved back to Canada. I moved to Boston and rented a six-room apartment in the same area my husband and I had been the year before. I enrolled my children in school and went on Aid to Dependent Children and no longer looked for work. I enjoyed the children and eagerly got up to make them a hot breakfast and to pack their school lunches. I was not good at managing a food budget; as a result, the day before the Aid To Dependent Children check arrived the cupboard was bare. I made the kids bean sandwiches to take to school, and for supper I made them luskinakin (flour and water biscuits), and potato soup. Despite these shortcomings, it was a nice life.

My experience with my husband in the city the previous year did not adequately prepare me for the situation I was now in, as I had the full responsibility of caring for myself and the nine children. In the beginning I was confident. However, as time passed I became less sure. I got homesick, a feeling I could not instantly identify. I'd left the reserve in haste, as if fleeing from something. From what, I did not know. Much later I found out what values I'd left behind. The reserve was where I had a sense of belonging. It was where I made connections to the earth, and to the people. I missed speaking my language.

It is strange to say, but I had a brother and sister living in the city. My brother was an alcoholic and lived in the streets. My sister was younger than I and lived in another area of the city and I did not see her.

I thought briefly of returning home to the reserve. The thought went out just as quickly as it came, for images of what reservation life was like then came vividly back. I speak only for myself and this is what I say: In the early thirties, reservation life was like death. People lived without hope. Indian agents assigned to the reserve did not speak of human rights, but preferred to keep us in bondage. Invisible boundaries—like a barbed wire fence—discrimination, and racist attitudes kept tribal people isolated. Fear hounded our thoughts and actions and clouded our existence and spiritual life. These elements were inoculated into our psyches as if born to it. It was a conditional process that affected our total being and left us with a lethargy we could not explain. We were bred to this process and could not in reality escape. The Indian agent, under the aegis of the federal government, ruled and controlled our lives. We lived in fear of the directives. I remember now, too, how in 1956 my husband and I had made the attempt to break free from reservation life. Some people did not flee and lived through the changes that eventually came to the reserves in Canada.

I'd been back in the city of Boston for a year when I became homesick. It hit me suddenly on a hot and steamy day as I was walking by myself at the neighborhood shopping center. It was a low blow. As a cloud of darkness penetrated my being, I heard music. It was loud and blared out from a neighborhood bar. I heard it over the ruckus the fire engines and ambulances made as they went blowing their sirens down the dusty streets. I stopped to listen. The music fascinated me, and it was as if it compelled me to enter. I hadn't been a drinker until then, but I thought that maybe I would go inside and have myself a beer.

I got my courage up and walked into the darkened bar. I couldn't see where the hell I was going. I sank into a booth and lit a cigarette. My hand shook. The waitress came over and I ordered a beer. Well, that is what started the whole damn thing. The disease, I mean. I became an alcoholic. It started off so innocently. When my eyes adjusted to the light, I took a quick look around the room. Men were standing at the bar holding glasses in hand. They were watching a baseball game on TV, and were rooting for Mickey Mantle to make a home-run. He did. Then all hell broke loose as they screamed and shouted. A middle-aged woman sitting alone across from me stared blankly into her glass.

I felt a dreadful feeling of isolation as I sipped the cold brew. As it happened, that day my life turned around, for I met in the bar the men and women of the neighborhood. For the most part they were of Irish descent and cheerfully welcomed me with their Irish Blarney. (I do not blame them for what happened to me.) Up until that time I had never known what a compliment was, nor had I ever been praised for anything I ever did. No one had ever noticed what I looked like or what I wore. Now all the attention I got from my new-found friends turned my head and gave me a such heady feeling that I puffed and preened in all the goodness that I felt.

As I became more confident and more adjusted to city life, the feelings of homesickness left. I began to go out evenings to the neighborhood bar, leaving my oldest daughter to tend to her brothers and sisters.

One evening, I overheard people talking about a bar that Native

American Indians frequented. I thought to myself, I will go next weekend to the inner city and seek it out. I wanted to meet up with my fellow Indians and to speak my language in the worst way. I wanted to hear what was happening back on the reserve, to hear news about family and friends.

The next week I was in a joyous mood as I made plans for the up-coming weekend. I was in a tizzy as I ran around the neighborhood. I went to the local beauty parlor and had my hair teased and fluffed up high in the latest fashion (bouffant style). I bought a new silk dress; it was the color blue. I bought new high-heeled shoes. That night after I got dressed up I looked in the mirror and was amazed at how I looked. I asked myself, "*Wow!* Where have I been all my life?" My black hair was soft and silky. I had a fair complexion;my figure was slim and trim. I had twelve kids, you know, and had just come through a ten-year period of hand washing diapers. Non-stop! I was twenty-eight years old.

I located the bar in the skid row section of the city that night and was shocked to find it filled with skid-row people. I was to find out that the bar was the meeting place for Indians in the city who gathered there to find family members and to find out news from home. Despite the fact that I sat beside baggy-eyed, pissy pants people, I had a good time that night: I met people who had just come down from Canada and I spoke in Micmac to them—my language!

The disease of alcoholism that I was suddenly hit with was subtle, for what values I held vanished as the first impact of the disease washed over me. I thought I was living for the first time. I was free. I'd lived a reservation life and was totally unaware of how conditioned I had been to it, and now, without realizing it, I was in the unknown territory of alcoholism.

I began dropping in at the neighborhood bar after I did my chores at the supermarket. The Saturday night drinking parties I had in my home extended to weekends. My children grew up in this atmosphere. I thought they attended school regularly; however, I found out some of them played hooky. My youngest child got himself in trouble with the law. He rang a fire alarm so often they traced him, and it was then that I was brought to the attention of the Children's Social Services. The agency's social workers investigated me and my home.

One gray, blustery morning I awakened early to hear the wind blowing hard against the window pane. Someone then began beating against my kitchen door. I opened it . . . and found the city child welfare workers standing there. They had a court order with them to take my children from me and place them in foster homes. I'd been charged by the courts and been found guilty of being an unfit mother. I fell into a chair and covered my head. They collected my nine kids ranging from six to fifteen and took them out to a waiting car.

I was stunned. What had I done? Back home on the reserve children ran free. Families took an interest in the children whenever a family was in need. The courts of the social workers did not offer any solutions or other options for me to consider. They just came and took the children. No one encouraged me, or advised me as how to get my children back, nor did they confront me with my problems with alcoholism. There was no one or any place I could turn to for help.

I moved to a rooming-house. The small room had a single burner hot plate in it, which I used to make coffee and heat up an occasional can of soup.

It was a dismal place. The hall that led to the bathroom was lit by a dim light bulb hanging down on a scraggly cord, and was shared by six other roomers. I found the changes I had to make unbearable. I worked nights in a factory and continued to drink every weekend. The disease of alcoholism increased rapidly in me as each weekend drinking bout became more severe. My physical condition deteriorated and I soon found myself unable to work. My mind was filled with anxiety, remorse and pain. I did not think of leaving the city and returning to the reserve without my children. I was desperate.

It was like fate or something, but it was about that time that I heard from a friend I hadn't heard from in years. This friend had become concerned about his problem drinking and joined a self-help group, and he invited me to come to the meetings with him. In the early stages of my recovery from alcoholism, I worked in a factory and attended meetings every night, and visited the children on weekends.

In the fifties and sixties the influx of tribal people—mainly Micmac Indians from north of the border—to Boston had begun on a large scale. At that time in Indian history tribal members were conditioned to be fearful of anyone with authority. As a result of their apprehension, the people often went without assistance or without services they might otherwise have obtained.

In 1972 the Boston Indian Council opened a multi-service center to provide services for a group of people who had, in fact, been overlooked or neglected by the social agencies of the city.

I volunteered to work at the agency, but was offered a paying job there as a receptionist. In 1972, I attended a general high school equivalency program at Roxbury Junior College, which I completed that year. I changed jobs at the center as well, and began to work as a teacher's aid. I enrolled in a one-year college program to study early childhood development. As I went along in the course I found it too painful as it showed, I thought, my own inadequacies as a mother. I could not be objective. I transferred out of the course and pursued the study of alcoholism. I changed jobs again and went from a children's aide to an outreach worker in the Indian Child Welfare Program.

In this position as a representative of the organization, and a court advocate, I was authorized to help Native American Indian mothers through the legal system. I returned children who been taken into custody by the court and placed in non-Indian foster homes to family members and/or to the reservation. I worked in this position for several years.

I gained control over my life, and made life choices. My children, were now five years older. They came home. Some stopped briefly with me before they ventured off on their own.

I became director of a halfway house for Native Americans. The house was a fourteen-bed facility and provided alcoholism treatment for Native Americans of the Northeast region. I stayed in the position for eight years, then returned to Canada.

Barbara Namias

5 ～

Barbara's Story

Barbara A. Namias has been director of the Indian Health Program at the Native American Indian Community Center of Boston for the past fifteen years. She is from the Snipe clan of the Mohawk Nation and is an enrolled member on the St. Regis (Akwesasne) Reservation in northern New York State. The Mohawks living at St. Regis south of the St. Lawrence River are part of a total community of over 10,000 that also occupies the Akwesasne Reserve in the Canadian provinces of Quebec and Ontario. Because the international boundary separates the Akwesasne Mohawk community, several governmental bodies have jurisdiction. Separate elected tribal councils govern the American and Canadian parts of the reservation. However, the traditionalist Akwesasne Longhouse does not recognize the artificial division and continues to speak for all Akwesasne Mohawks. The United States, Canadian, state, provincial, and county governments also claim various jurisdiction.

Barbara's maternal grandparents were Mohawk, although her grandfather also had Oneida forebears. Both grandparents attended Thomas' Indian School in New York State and then Carlisle Indian School in Pennsylvania. After the United States entered World War I, Carlisle was closed and converted into a training base for the troops going to Europe. Barbara's grandfather joined the navy, while her grandmother was scheduled to be transferred to Mt. Pleasant Indian School in Michigan. She never went there, however; in the fall she disappeared into the Iroquois community in Syracuse, New York. There she met up with her husband-to-be several years later.

Barbara tells her own story:

After my grandparents married they began a transient lifestyle, following the skilled ironworker trade. My grandfather was an ironworker, and the family moved frequently. Their three children were born in three different cities: Syracuse, Philadelphia, and Binghamton, New York. Eventually they settled in New York City. Shortly thereafter the Department of Social Services became involved with the family, and their three children were placed in a Catholic home in nearby Nyack, New York. Alcoholism was at the root of the family's dysfunction.

My mother was fourteen when she and her two siblings were returned to the custody of their mother. But the home still remained dysfunctional. My mother left to marry when she was nineteen. Later, after she separated from my father, she brought her own two children back to her mother's home, where we remained for the next two years.

Meanwhile, Grandfather was living a carefree lifestyle and was in and out of our lives for the remainder of his life. He left the ironworker's trade and worked at sewing awnings, which provided him with a steady income. He visited us often and when he did he told my cousin Sam and me stories. Holding a can of beer in his hand, he relished the telling of those stories. We were a captive audience. But there was one theme he was also serious about, and he repeated it over and over again. That was: the wrongdoers of this country would get their due, and we would get the land back. He would go on to tell Sam and me, "That's why you have to stay strong and not forget who you are." Sam was three and a half years older than I. Mother had taken him in when he was two and raised him as her own. I had a younger brother, James, but he was three and a half years younger than I and wasn't interested in hearing Grandfather's stories.

We left Grandmother's home after two years to live in a small apartment in the Bronx. To reach it we had to walk down an alley littered with garbage. Mother was a single parent and we found out that we were the first family on the block to receive welfare. These conditions caused an uproar in the neighborhood and the kids were forbidden to play with us. Mother was pretty compared to the other women of the neighborhood. She had long, black, silky hair and dark eyes; her complexion was lightly tanned. She was the subject of the women's gossip, but their husbands, aware of her beauty, never spoke an unkind word about her.

Meanwhile, Grandfather continued to visit, as did Sam's

mother, Louise, and my Uncle Buddy. Louise was emotionally unstable and as a result there would be havoc in the apartment whenever she came to visit. Fights broke out. One time I was trapped in the center of a melee and to get free of it I jumped out the window and hung by my hands before I dropped to the ground.

Sam and I were enrolled in Our Lady of Mercy School. He got into first grade the year we moved to our new home. I had to wait another year before I started school as the kindergarten class was filled up and Mother did not want to send me to the public school kindergarten. At the Catholic school I attended I was taught that Mohawks were savages, that they had burned the hands of a priest and had tied him to a tree when he attempted to save their souls. They also said the devil had taken hold of the savages and wouldn't let them go. But God is good and looked kindly on Mohawks. Kateri Tekakwitha, a Mohawk girl, was special because when she died her skin color turned from brown to lily white, after which she became known as "The Lily of the Mohawks." She died young, but her soul was saved and she saw God when she died.

The kids on our block made fun of our family because we were Indian. One kid's father called our apartment a "wigwam" all of the time. He referred to my hard-drinking family as "crazy Indians." The neighborhood kids who were the same age as Sammy took off his shirt one summer day and held him across a hot metal mailbox to make his skin turn red, like a real Indian's—a "redskin." The day it happened, Mother had a few beers. When she heard about the incident she took off after the boys, yelling and throwing stones at them. The kids were busting their guts with laughter as they fled from her anger. As fate would have it, my Uncle Buddy visited us that afternoon. He was a big—6-foot-6-inch—person and weighed about 240 pounds. He heard about the incident and somehow managed to grab two of the boys; he shook them hard, then brought them back to their parents' home. One of the boys' father had been drinking also, and he and my Uncle Buddy got into a fist fight. Uncle Buddy could fight! They didn't call him "the Big Indian" for nothing. He sure kicked ass that day!

Family life was never dull (to put it mildly!). Our identity as a family was strong. It included my mother, grandmother, Uncle Buddy, Aunt Louise, and Grandfather. We always celebrated holidays, and birthdays, too. One time Grandfather got me an Oakley rifle. At Christmas, Grandmother bought us children shoes. Mother bought our clothes. Mother eventually worked at Schrafft's as a waitress but always had time to make Halloween costumes, have birthday parties, and cook Thanksgiving dinners.

I graduated from a Catholic high school in 1968 and entered City College of New York's Manhattan campus. I excelled in all my classes. I entered college under a minority student higher education program, but when the stipends for higher education came to an abrupt end, my education also ended. (Years later, in 1982, I received a master's degree in education from Cambridge College in Cambridge, Massachusetts.) I went to live on the reservation and while there volunteered my time working on *Akwesasne Notes*, an Indian newspaper whose office was located within St. Regis, or *Akwesasne*. (In Mohawk, the area where the Nation is located is called *Akwesasne*, which translates to "Land Where the Partridge Drums.")

After a two-and-a-half-year period on the St. Regis Reservation I returned to New York City, where I worked for the American Indian Community House. Over the next ten years I was to receive an education in Native American issues and legal rights. It began when, in 1978, I applied for and was awarded a two-year internship with the Institute for the Development of Indian Law, based in Washington, D.C. I was there from 1978 to 1980.

Those were the seventies, the time of the takeover of the Bureau of Indian Affairs office, Wounded Knee, and the enactment of major pro-Indian legislation: the American Indian Health Care Improvement Act (1976), the Indian Child Welfare Act (1978), and the American Indian Religious Freedom Act (1978). Until the mid-twentieth century, many policies established by the early federal government for Native American Indian tribes had remained in place. One policy prohibited Indian ceremonial rituals, while others continued to impede the free exercise of native religion. Acknowledging this fact, the United States Congress passed the American Indian Religious Freedom Act, signed into law by President Carter on August 11, 1979.

Major court decisions were handed down during this period as well. *U.S. v. Washington State* (or the Boldt decision of 1974), determined that in their traditional fishing areas Indian fishermen were entitled to share equally in the harvest of fish with non-Indian commercial fishermen. A battle had been waged between commercial fishermen and the Puget Sound tribes for years, but now the tribes' right to fish and manage fisheries under existing treaties had been upheld. The original decision by District Court Judge

George Boldt was affirmed by the United States Supreme Court in a related case, *Washington v. Washington State Commercial Passenger Fishing Vessel Association* (1979). I was actually sitting in the courtroom during the presentation of the case. It was a memorable experience in my life, one where I actually experienced a natural high as the arguments continued. When the Supreme Court handed down its decision that summer, it was great—the Court had found in favor of the tribe!

I grew up in the Bronx with a close-knit family who instilled in me the concept of an extended family system in which each member had a role and a responsibility to see that others in the family would have a little better life than they had. It's the Tribal Clan system applied to an urban setting.

When I reach retirement age, I would like to look back upon a work experience that promoted urban community health and opportunities for growth and advancement in both community and individuals.

Helen Manning

6 🌾

Helen's Story

*F*ive miles off the coast of southeastern Massachusetts, south of the heel of Cape Cod, lies the island of Martha's Vineyard. Of the six towns on the island, Gay Head is the smallest. Situated on a peninsula at the westernmost tip, it contains only 18 square miles or approximately 3400 acres. Gay Head's outstanding natural feature is its famous clay cliffs, rare in their rich and varied colors. The town is home to the Gay Head Wampanoags, whose presence there is first documented in the sixteenth century. Today, more than 800 names appear on the tribal rolls. Three hundred Wampanoags live on the island itself, while the rest can be found elsewhere throughout the world.

Helen Manning, an enrolled member of the tribe, was born in 1919. Her mother was a teacher who studied art at Columbia University in New York City. Her father was a Wampanoag who traced his ancestry back seven generations. A successful entrepreneur in Gay Head, he owned a commercial trap-fishing business as well as a restaurant on the famous cliffs.

Helen Manning narrates her own story:

When I was six months old, we went to Washington, D.C. to visit my mother's family and to show off me, their first grandchild. That family visit initiated a family pattern of leaving Gay Head before Christmas and returning in March or April. As a result of living in two different basic environments, culturally and socially I found I was experiencing the best of two worlds. This pattern remained in place until I was seven years old.

I attended my first powwow in 1929, and in the years that followed, a yearly pageant held by the Wampanoags of Gay Head. That was where I first heard the legends of Martha's Vineyard.

Dancing, singing, and community participation were involved. A medicine man was in attendance. Then the yearly pageants stopped. Community participation in Indian rituals did not occur again until 1944.

When I was eight my parents sent me to the District of Columbia to live with my grandmother. They felt that the educational opportunities there were superior to the one-room schoolhouse at Gay Head. All of my undergraduate studies as well were done in Washington, including teacher training at Miner Teachers' College. I later received my master's degree in elementary education from New York University.

Up until 1941 I enjoyed this wonderful "best of two worlds" because I always came to Gay Head for the summer. My parents ran an inn there. During those summers I went clamming, fished for lobster, and picked blueberries, huckleberries, blackberries, and swamp apples. In the fall I enjoyed the Cranberry Festival. Most families at that time had chickens and usually a pig in their backyards.

My maternal grandmother was a teacher, my aunt was a teacher, and my mother was a teacher. It was an unwritten understanding that I, too, would be a teacher. Needless to say, I wanted to be anything but a teacher! Upon graduation from Teachers' College, I took the required exam for teaching in the District of Columbia and flunked! This was during the Depression and I had to find a job.

My first job was at the Bureau of Engraving and Printing, where paper money is printed. It was a factory. From there I went first to the Children's Bureau in the Labor Department, then to the War Labor Board during World War II, and finally to the Orientalia Division of, the Library of Congress. Eventually I took a job as assistant to the Dean of Women at Fisk University in Nashville, Tennessee.

In Nashville I met my first husband, who was studying dentistry at Meharry Medical School. We were married in 1946 and moved back to Washington, where I again took the teachers' exam. This time I passed it! I was appointed to Birney School in Anacostia, where I taught first grade for seven years.

The summer my husband and I divorced, I came back to the Island for a visit. While there, I head of a job opening at the one-room school at Gay Head. I applied, got the job, and held the position for thirteen years.

Being a teacher in a one-room school that included grades 1

through 6 was an experience every teacher should have. It was an even more wonderful experience for me because, of the sixteen children attending, all but three of my pupils were Native Americans, predominantly Gay Head Wampanoag.

In 1968, when enrollment had been reduced to five children in four grades, the school was closed for lack of pupils. I was transferred to Oak Bluffs Elementary School, also on Martha's Vineyard, where I taught remedial reading to kindergarten through fourth-grade students and did testing and programming for students with learning disabilities.

When I first started teaching at Gay Head School I had an interesting experience at a meeting held before school opened. The teachers at the meeting were sharing experiences of our various social studies programs. I mentioned that the tribal group on the island was studying its history and tribal contributions to the development of Martha's Vineyard and went on to say, "We plan to involve the whole community." "Oh, my!" said one of the teachers. "Won't that interfere with completing your social studies text?" Of course, the text had not word in it about Martha's Vineyard or of the Wampanoags. The school superintendent was at the meeting and he agreed with the teacher. I was shocked—painfully so—to hear island teachers and supervisors say they were not the least bit interested in learning about the Wampanoags and their contributions to the island. All they wanted to address was what the non-Indian people contributed to the island.

That meeting did not stop my enthusiasm for having Wampanoag culture entered into the school curriculum. I find it very satisfactory that today teachers are imploring the tribal council for information to teach more about the Wampanoag culture. Now, teachers are anxious to have members of the Wampanoag community come to talk to the classes. This makes the Wampanoag students feel good about themselves and helps to let the non-Indians know to what extent another culture contributed to the making of this community. It builds mutual respect. I retired from teaching at Oak Bluffs Elementary School in 1984.

Ten years earlier, in 1974, I was part of a group of Gay Head Wampanoags who formed the Wampanoag Tribal Council. The group sought legal expertise and filed a land suit asking the town for lands formerly meant for Wampanoag people when Gay Head was predominantly an Indian town. (Wampanoags are now a minority in the town.) We asked for the Common Lands, the Herring Creek, and the Cliffs. We wanted them returned to the Wampanoags and not under the jurisdiction of the town. The Taxpayers' Organization, made up mostly of summer residents, fought the transfer. The land was not formally returned until 1988. The tribe had already received federal recognition in 1987.

This situation led to my interest in town government. I ran for and was elected Selectman in 1974. I was also elected to the Martha's Vineyard Commission, a regional land-use planning agency for the island. I was also on the Conservation Commission and the Museum Committee. For three years I served on the Tribal Council.

While living with my grandmother in Washington, I attended Sunday school at a Baptist church where grandmother was enrolled. Later, when I returned to the Island to live, I attended a liberal Baptist church which both Wampanoags and Islanders attended.

Now, on mornings when I come out of my house to stand on the cliffs overlooking the ocean, I feel close to Indian teachings. I sense the presence of spiritual guides. . . I know they are with me. I know, too, that when I walk along the beach that I am walking on sacred and spiritual ground.

Presently I am involved with the revitalization of our language. During the centuries of cultural assimilation, we have lost many of the traditions and cultural practices, including oral language, that were once passed from generation to generation. With the oral traditions and skills either lost or close to extinction, our people are struggling to restore a spiritual connection through the revival of traditional cultural practices and activities that will begin to enable our people to really "Be Indian."

The Legend of Moshup, as retold by Helen Manning

For many thousands of years Wampanoag Indians lived here on Martha's Vineyard in a series of villages consisting of circular, bark-covered wigwams called *wetus*. They hunted mammals on land and sea and collected shellfish and plants, fish and fowl, even though the Indians here had contact with Europeans since the fifteenth and sixteenth centuries. Ships from all over the world came to trade furs, sassafras roots, and fish, and to find new places to locate their homes and begin communities. Bartholomew Gosnold, who arrived in the spring of 1602, was the first explorer to keep a record of information about Martha's Vineyard, Nantucket, Cape Cod, and the

Elizabeth Islands and the people who lived here.

Here on Martha's Vineyard Moshup was recognized as the maker of all things. Gay Head oral tradition states that the first Indians to populate Martha's Vineyard found a giant named Moshup. He was already living in his cave when the first Wampanoag came with his dog to Martha's Vineyard on a cake of ice. The chunk of ice had been carried out from the mainland and despite his efforts was driven to the island of *Noepe* (the Indian name for Martha's Vineyard). The Wampanoag Indians (also called Pokanokets) knew of the existence of this island but had never visited it before since they believed it to be inhabited by Harbormonk, a feared evil spirit, and Cheepi, a mischievous one. When the lost man began to explore the island, he found it inhabited by a monstrous giant who lived in the den at the end of the island. This was at the western end, which was called *Aquinnah* then and is called Gay Head today. The giant was taller than the tallest tree, a coronopeia, and was as large around as a spread from a fully grown pine. He excelled in all feats of strength and bravery because he was said to be endowed with supernatural powers. His great prowess in war and sport was often attributed to magic.

Moshup told the stranger that he had once lived on the mainland but had waded to the island in pursuit of huge birds which had been carrying away the children of his tribe. He found the bones of all the children under a great tree. A little farther on he found the nest of the bird with seven of its young. After a long battle Moshup succeeded in killing these monstrous birds. He was so fatigued by this battle that he lay down to rest. During his fitful sleep he had a dream telling him he must not leave the island. When he awoke he had a strong urge to smoke but had no tobacco. He looked around and found some small green leaves on a vine on the ground. He filled his pipe with the Poke which our people sometimes use today in place of tobacco. Moshup then seated himself on the hills and began to smoke. The smoke spread over the surface of the sea and it became misty—the beginning of the fog, which even today obscures Noepe at times.

For many moons Moshup wandered ever eastward until he came at last to low marshy lands. There, weary and worn, he dragged his great toes, thereby creating the chain of islands known today as the Elizabeth Islands. Wishing to make a complete separation from those with whom he had lived in such turmoil, he again dragged his great toes, permitting the waters of the ocean to rush in and surround the land we now know as Martha's Vineyard. Thus did Moshup separate his people from their somber way of life, choosing as a home for them the colorful headlands of Gay Head, where they erected their wigwams and settled in this hollow which in time came to be known as Moshup's Den.

Moshup's family consisted of his wife Squant, their twelve stalwart sons, and their twelve beautiful daughters. Squant was broad but finely proportioned, with coal black hair that she wore over her face. The reason for this was given by those who beheld her face when her veil was lifted and told to us by our forefathers in tones of awe: Squant's eyes were square! They had been cut and shaped that way by an enemy who one day found her asleep on the marsh. Thus, her beautiful hair was used to cover her hideous deformity. Some say it was Cheepie's work.

Even in those long ago days, feeding a family the size of Moshup's was a problem. But, behold mighty Moshup as he stands on the edge of the cliffs, seeking with his keen eyes the whale that would provide the food. (In those times whales came close to shore, for they had not yet learned to fear pursuit by human beings. Later, whaling became an industry adapted from the Indian's first crew efforts. Many Gay Head men sailed the world on early whaling ships.)

Now Moshup makes his catch and hauls it in to be prepared by his wife and daughters for the evening meal. Blood from this slaughter of the leviathan of the deep stained some of our cliffs a dark red that may be seen today. Whale teeth, shark teeth, and quahog fossils still found on the cliffs testify that the refuse used from Moshup's table was discarded close by his wigwam. Mighty trees were needed to kindle the fires on which the whales were cooked. Day by day the nearby forest was stripped, which no doubt accounts for the present scarcity of trees in Gay Head. Moshup did not consume all the bounty himself but, with a benevolent hand, often supplied the other Indians with food already cooked. To facilitate the catching of these fish he threw many large stones into the sea so that they landed at intervals convenient for him to walk upon. This is now called Devil's Bridge. On summer evenings Moshup would sit at his enormous doorway smoking his great pewter leaf, as the Indians called his pipe. In good humor at close of day and well content with his lot, Moshup often gave kindly advice to his people, who brought their problems to him for his consideration.

A young girl had been sent by her mother to gather leaves along the edge of Split Mountain. There she met a brave from the Sachem of Takemmy. When their eyes met, there was no question in their hearts that they had fallen in love. When the girl went home and told her parents she fell into deep sadness. Marriage between the two was not possible. Her parents were too poor to provide the gifts of marriage without which no Indian ceremony could be performed. The next day she went back to the pond and told her lover. He was steadfast, however. Love like theirs came from the heavens. They would go and seek help from Moshup, the giant god of their people.

They walked to Moshup's Den in the cliffs of Aquinnah where Moshup had made his home. They told him of their sadness and of their love for each other. Moshup listened and told them that at sunset he would be at Chappaquiddick. He would give them his answer then. The young couple hurried to Nunepog and swam across the water to Chappaquiddick. They could see the smoke from Moshup's pipe rising in the air. They hurried toward him.

Moshup seemed lost in thought, his eyes gazing on far-off seas. He was silent for so long that the young girl became frightened. The sun was about to set and Moshup had said nothing. She begged Moshup to speak. Still looking at the sea, Moshup stood up and emptied the bowl of his giant pipe. A wind from the water blew by and carried the ashes seaward. As they floated into the sea, the ocean water hissed and foamed, and steam rolls, like silver clouds, rose into the sky. The young couple watched as an island took shape in the distant sea.

Moshup pointed. "There is your wedding gift," he said. "There you may live in peace and prosperity." The young lovers fell to his feet with thankfulness. As they opened their eyes they saw a canoe on the shore.

Moshup smiled and waved to the young lovers as they paddled to Nantucket.

Sweet grass

Sweet grass is a tall, wild grass, growing in areas of the U.S. northwest and southern Canada. It has long been a sacred plant for Native Americans. The dried leaves and flowers are woven into baskets, and the long, sweet-musty scented leaves are braided and burned in purification ceremonies. The smoke from sweet grass encourages positive influences and carries prayers up to the Creator.

Once common, sweet grass has become rare due to development, cattle-grazing, and wheat growing. Native Americans in the northern plains have tried to protect remaining fields.